love★com

Story & Art by
Aya Nakahara

love★com

contents 8

The Story So Far. . .

Risa and Ôtani are their class's lopsided comedy duo...except that Risa's fallen in love with Ôtani! She finally works up the courage to tell him how she feels, only to be totally rejected. Even so, she keeps trying to change his mind, and it looks like her efforts have paid off: he kisses her!! Or did he? Because the next day, he doesn't remember a thing about it...This is too much for Risa, and she decides she's through with him. She starts a fan club for dreamy new teacher Mr. Maitake (a.k.a. Mighty) and throws herself into some serious fandom...and Ôtani gets awfully grumpy. And when Risa reminds him that she's decided to quit being in love with him, he tells her not to! And then, on her birthday, he gets her a present and kisses her for real. So it looks like things're finally working out for Risa, except...

♥ To really get all the details, check out Lovely Complex Vol. 1-7, available at bookstores everywhere!!

love★com

Lovely★Complex
ATSUSHI ŌTANI
Birthday:March 25
Constellation:Aries
Blood type:A
Birthplace:Osaka

8

Story & Art by
Aya Nakahara

LOVELY

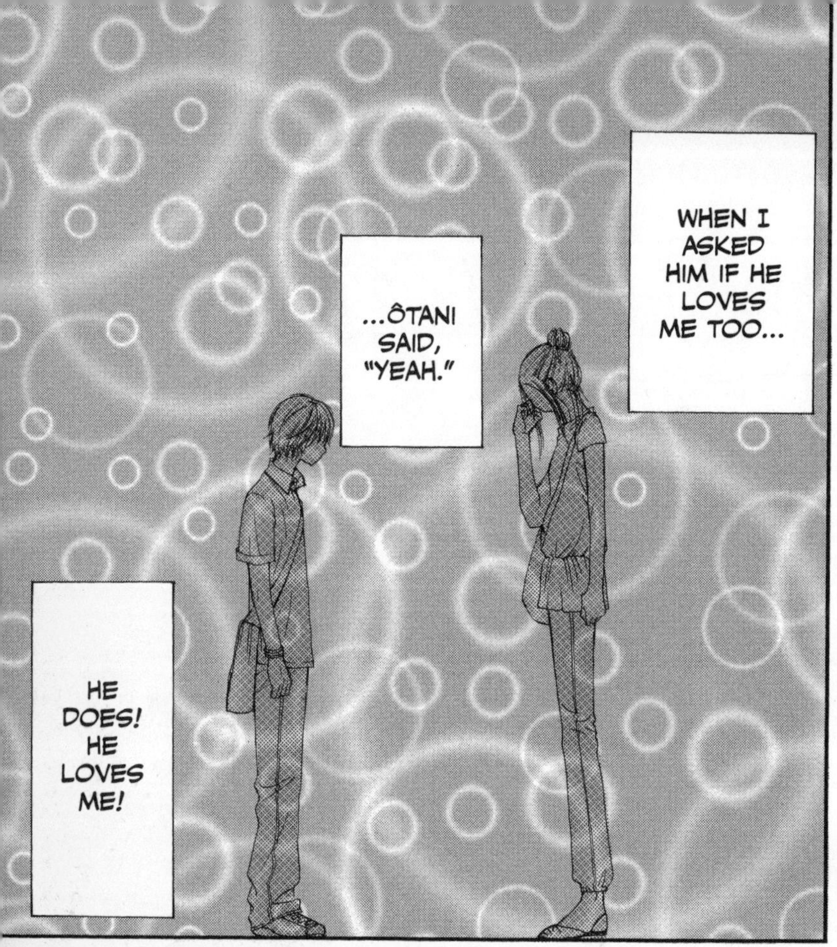

WHEN I ASKED HIM IF HE LOVES ME TOO...

...ÔTANI SAID, "YEAH."

HE DOES! HE LOVES ME!

CHAPTER 29

IT SURE WAS A LONG AND ROCKY ROAD.
I PUT A LOT OF HARD WORK INTO IT, I REALLY DID.
AND NOW, FOR THE FIRST TIME IN MY LIFE, I'M GOING OUT WITH SOMEONE.
STARTING TODAY...
...I FINALLY GET TO HAVE A LOVE LIFE!
WHAT ARE YOU, A MORON?!

YOU DON'T EVEN KNOW HOW TO WRING OUT A RAG? YOU DIP!
WHAT'RE YOU TALKING ABOUT? I'M WRINGING IT OUT!!
YOU WRING IT OUT OVER THE BUCKET, STUPID! YOU'RE GETTING WATER ALL OVER THE PLACE!!
SO WHAT'S THE BIG DEAL? I'LL JUST WIPE IT UP LATER!!
...
Splash
FORGET IT, THEY'RE GONNA BE THERE ALL DAY. LET'S GO.
WHAT'RE THEY DOING?
THEY HAVE TO CLEAN THE CLASSROOM AS PUNISHMENT FOR HAVING THE WORST GRADES OF EVERYBODY IN SUMMER SCHOOL.
WHEN ARE THEY EVER GOING TO GET TOGETHER, THOSE TWO?
MAYBE THEY'RE ALREADY TOGETHER, WHO KNOWS?
WHAAT? COME ON.
...
Who cares how I wring out the rag, anyway? What are you, my mother-in-law?

LOOK, I JUST WANT TO GET THIS OVER WITH AND GET THE HECK OUTTA HERE.
DON'T GIVE US ONE MORE THING TO DO.
WELL, WHAT I'M SAYING IS...
...IS THAT HOW YOU TALK TO THE WOMAN YOU LOVE?!
...what's with the big attitude all of a sudden?
OH, JUST A LITTLE PAYBACK FOR ALL THE TIMES YOU SAID IT TO ME.
"YEAH"!
?
YEAH, WHAT?
THAT WAS YOU, ACTUALLY.

YOU LOVE ME TOO, DON'T YOU?
YEAH.
DWOO HOO HOO HOOO.
YOU ARE THE TOTAL PITS!!
WHO'S THE ONE WHO WAS WEEPING AND WAILING ABOUT HOW NUTS SHE IS ABOUT ME, HUH?!
I LOVE YOU SO MUCH.
HEY!
DIRECT HIT
WELL, WHAT ABOUT YOU, MAKING A BIG DEAL ABOUT WHO YOU KISS AND WHO YOU DON'T KISS?!
YOU THINK I GO AROUND DOING STUFF LIKE
DIRECT HIT
WELL...

WHAT'RE YOU DOING?
Just clean up and go, will ya?

...WELL, WHAT IT IS, IS...

SO YEAH, WE'RE FINALLY GOING OUT...

...AND I'M REALLY HAPPY AND EXCITED ABOUT IT...

Bye-bye!

Ha ha ha!

...BUT THERE'S JUST ONE PROBLEM.

mween

mween

mween

HOW DO WE CHANGE GEARS?
TOK
TOK
TOK

SO, HEY!

THANK GOD SUMMER SCHOOL'S OVER, HUH? NOW WE CAN FINALLY HAVE SOME FUN!
WELL, WE HARDLY HAVE ANY VACATION LEFT.

ZWONK
Why do you have to be such a downer, Ôtani...?

JUST TELLING IT LIKE IT IS. STILL GOT A TON OF HOMEWORK TO DO.

OH YEAH...
I MEAN, I JUST PASSED THE ÔTANI TEST, WHICH HAS GOTTA BE HARDER THAN ANY EXAMS WE GET AT SCHOOL...
I WANNA CELEBRATE!
HEH HEH...
HEY, ONCE SCHOOL STARTS AGAIN WE'RE GONNA HAVE TO STUDY PRETTY HARD, SO...
...LET'S GO DO SOMETHING FUN WHILE WE STILL GOT THE TIME FOR IT.
WHO CARES... ABOUT STUFF LIKE THAT...?

YEAH, TOTALLY!
I'LL CALL NOBU AND SEE IF...
DON'T, STUPID.
HEH?

I MEANT JUST US TWO.
WHAAAAAT?
JUST US TWO-OOO?
WHAT?! WHAT'RE YOU SCREAMING ABOUT? WE'VE GONE OUT ALONE TONS OF TIMES!!
YEAH, BUT!!
I MEAN!!
WHAT?!

THIS IS GONNA BE A DATE!!
...
...YOU GOT A PROBLEM WITH THAT?
NO, SIR!
SHWEEN
SHWEEN
RIGHT!
OH
MY
GOD!! A DATE!! OMIGOD!!

SO OKAY, WE *HAVE* GONE OUT ALONE BEFORE, LOTS OF TIMES.
FWAP
FWAP
BUT THIS TIME'S TOTALLY DIFFERENT.
AAAAGH!!
WHAT DO I WEAR?!
TOSS
This?! Or this?!
THIS TIME, IT'S A DATE. A REAL DATE.
OOOH
SO I AM SUPER-PSYCHED!!
VROOOOM

blah
blah
blah
WAAAH!
blah
SORRY SORRY SORRY!
blah
THAT'S OKAY, I LOVE STANDING AROUND TRAIN STATIONS.
blah
HANH HANH
I'M REALLY SORRY ...!
WELL, WHATEVER. I'M TOTALLY USED TO IT BY NOW.
WHADDAYA MEAN, USED TO IT BY NOW?
LIKE I'M ALWAYS LATE OR SOME-THING!!
WELL, ONE OUT OF THREE TIMES, AT LEAST. AND IT'S ALWAYS 'CUZ YOU OVERSLEPT TOO.
OH, LIKE YOU NEVER DO?!
I ONLY DO IT EVERY ONCE IN A WHILE, WHEN IT REALLY COUNTS! LIKE FOR OUR CLASS TRIP!
AND THAT'S BETTER?!

HEY! YOU MAKE ME WAIT AROUND ALL THIS TIME AND THEN START YELLING AT ME?!

URGH

BEG PARDON ...

ER...

ALLOW ME TO TREAT YOU TO SOME-THING TODAY...

HM. OKAY.

I AM SO LAME...

YOU'RE EARLY.

OH, NOT REALLY. I JUST GOT HERE!

THE PLAN WAS TO GET HERE FIRST AND DO THAT...

hfff

OH NO!

WHAT?

I FORGOT TO BRING MY PURSE.

YOU WHAT?!
FLUSTER
FLUSTER
I was in a huge hurry 'cuz I was late, so...

LET ME GO HOME AND GET...
WHAT AM I SUPPOSED TO DO, WAIT HERE ANOTHER HOUR? AND THEN WE'LL HAVE EVEN LESS TIME DOWNTOWN!
'Cuz you were totally late!

BUT MY MONEY AND EVERY-THING'S IN...
OH!
WHAT ?!

I FOUND SOME COINS IN MY POCKET. ♡
OH GREAT, THAT'S A HUGE HELP!!
WE CAN GO PLAY PACHINKO AROUND THE CORNER!!

SO LET ME GO HOME AND GET MY PURSE...
...

THAT'S OKAY.
I'LL GET EVERY-THING TODAY.
...SORRY ...
C'MON, LET'S GO.
KREEE
...OH GOD...
FORGET ABOUT HAVING A LOVE LIFE AFTER ALL.
KA-TUNK
KA-TUNK
KA-TUNK
KA-TUNK
AT THIS RATE, HE'S GOING TO TAKE BACK THAT "YEAH" AND TOTALLY DUMP ME.

KA-TUNK
I HAVE TO MAKE UP FOR THIS SOMEHOW! MAKE MYSELF LOOK GOOD!!
KA-TONK
KA-TUNK
WAAAAH!
...BUT HOW?!
HEY, KOIZUMI.
WHAT DO I DOOO?
Uh-huh...
WHOA! DID SOMEONE DIE OR SOME-THING?!
Well, I'm kind of dying... But, yeah?
THERE'S THIS PLACE I WANT TO CHECK OUT DOWNTOWN. MIND IF WE GO?
A PLACE YOU WANT TO CHECK OUT?
...?

1

Hello. Nakahara here. We're up to Volume 8!

Sooooo...
How are you, everybody?

As I write this, it's only June, but it's already super-hot out. I almost fainted when I went out for a few moments the other day, so I made a solemn pledge to myself to spend this summer holed up inside the house.

Like, was that really necessary? I'm always holed up inside the house anyway. hahahahahaha

Not to mention, who cares? Do you care? No. It's like, whatever!

But if you listen to people talking on the street, they're all talking about stuff nobody cares about, actually. Like,

"Gosh, it's crowded..."
"Man, it's hot..."
"Wow, what a beautiful day..."

Stuff anybody can see for themselves. You don't need to say it out loud!

WAS THIS PLACE HERE BEFORE?!
It's ¥100 for 15 minutes on any game in the whole joint!
IT JUST OPENED. THERE WAS THIS FLYER IN OUR MAILBOX ABOUT IT, AND I WAS LIKE, GOTTA CHECK IT OUT!
OMIGOD!! THIS IS SO COOL, ŌTANI!! YOU ARE A GENIUS!!
YAAAAY!!
I KNOW, HUH? GO AHEAD AND PLAY WHATEVER YOU WANT.
WAHOOOO
KA-CHEEEN
KA-CHAANK
WAHA-HOOO
WAHA-HOOO
YAHOOOO
FWAKKA
FWAKKA
FWAKKA
THWUNK
THWUNK
THWUNK
THWUNK
THWOKKA
THWOKKA
THWOKKA
WOOOH! ALL RIIIIGHT!! THIRD GAME IN A ROW!!
AAARGH! I WASN'T EVEN CLOSE THIS TIME!! YOU ARE TOO GOOD!

YOU HAVING A GOOD TIME?!
I'M HAVING A GREAT TIME!! I LOVE THIS PLACE!!
I KNEW YOU WOULD!!
WAHOOO
WHEN I SAW THE FLYER, AND ALL THE GAMES THEY GOT HERE, I WAS LIKE, KOIZUMI'S GONNA GO NUTS IN THIS PLACE! I JUST KNEW YOU'D LOVE IT.
...HE WAS THINKING ABOUT ME...
...ŌTANI ...
OKAY, ONE MORE TIME! AND THIS TIME I'M GONNA BEAT YOU!!
DADIDOO

OH, DAAA-AARN!

I LOST AGAAAIN!

GOOOSH, YOU ARE SOOO GOOOD! ♡

HEH, HEH. JUST MY LUCKY DAY, I GUESS.

ULP!! OF COURSE!!

YOU LOOK CUTER IF YOU LET THE GUY WIN!!

HEY, PAY ATTENTION. GAME'S ABOUT TO START.

ÔTANI PICKED THIS PLACE OUT FOR OUR FIRST DATE BECAUSE HE WAS THINKING ABOUT ME AND WHAT I'D ENJOY...

...AND WHAT DID I DO? I FORGOT MY PURSE AT HOME AND CAME LATE...

...AND THEN I PILED ON EVERY KILLER GAMING MOVE I KNOW TO BEAT HIM TO A PULP...

I SUCK. I AM THE TOTAL PITS...
GLOOOOOM
blah
blah
HAAAA-AANGH...
IF YOU'RE BORED OUTTA YOUR MIND, JUST SAY SO.
WAAAH!! NO!! THAT'S NOT WHAT THAT MEANT!!
I'M SORRY, ÔTANI...
OH. UH, THAT'S OKAY.

HEY, YOU WANNA PLAY PING-PONG NEXT? WHEN WE'RE DONE HERE?
...HEY, ÔTANI?
HM?
DID YOU GO ON A LOT OF DATES WITH YOUR OLD GIRLFRIEND?
BWOGH
WHERE'D *THAT* COME FROM?
WELL, IT'S JUST THAT...
...I'VE NEVER BEEN ON A DATE WITH ANYBODY BEFORE IN MY ENTIRE LIFE.
SO I DON'T KNOW WHAT I'M SUPPOSED TO DO.

BUT YOU SEEM REALLY USED TO IT, LIKE YOU GO OUT ON DATES ALL THE TIME. LIKE, THE WAY YOU PICKED THIS PLACE...

STOP TALKING ABOUT ME LIKE I'M MISTER SMOOTH OR SOME-THING!!

I ONLY PICKED THIS PLACE 'CUZ IT LOOKED LIKE A LOT OF FUN, AND I THOUGHT WE'D HAVE A GOOD TIME. WHAT'S THAT GOT TO DO WITH GOING ON DATES ALL THE TIME?

WELL, IT WAS PERFECT. YOU REALLY GRABBED ME BY THE HEART-STRINGS, ÔTANI.

MY, MY. SO I'VE GRABBED YOU BY THE HEART-STRINGS HAVE I?
YEAH.
IT'S NOT FAIR. I WANT TO GRAB *YOU* BY THE HEART-STRINGS, TOO.
SORRY, GIRL, BUT I'M NOT A PUSHOVER LIKE YOU ARE.

HEY.
OW!
NYAAARGH
I MUST'VE HIT MY HAND AGAINST SOME-THING. MY FINGER'S CUT.
GLEAM
HANG ON, I'VE GOT A BAND-AID YOU CAN PUT ON IT!
I JUST PUT SOME IN MY PURSE THE OTHER...
...day...
But I don't have my purse here...
WANNA CHECK YOUR POCKETS?
I SWEAR I MAKE MYSELF SICK. I AM SO DARN USELESS...

HEY, IT'S NO BIG DEAL. WHAT'S UP WITH YOU TODAY?
YOU'RE TRYING TOO HARD. JUST BE THE WAY YOU ALWAYS ARE.
...
BET IF THAT HAPPENED ON A DATE WITH HIS EX, SHE'D PRODUCE A BAND-AID *THAT FAST.* BET SHE CARRIES DOZENS OF THEM AROUND.
I MEAN, SHE WAS ONLY THE BASKET-BALL TEAM MANAGER.
AND SHE WAS SO CUTE TOO, THAT GIRL MAYU...
GUESS I SHOULDN'T KEEP COM-PARING MYSELF TO HER.
BET SHE'S SUPER-THOUGHT-FUL.
BUT I CAN'T HELP THINK-ING, ISN'T A LOSER LIKE THIS AFTER A CUTIE LIKE THAT...
A loser like this.
...KIND OF A LET-DOWN?
ZHGOOO

PHOOGH! MAN, AM I FULL!
TUNK
HERE, LET *ME* TAKE THAT!
KLATTER
KTONK
KWIP
!
KA-SHANK
SCATTER
KRASH
SPLASH
SCATTER

DON'T WORRY ABOUT IT. I'LL CLEAN IT UP.
YOU CAN JUST LEAVE IT RIGHT THERE!
I'm...
...really sorry...
It's okay.
YOU BIG KLUTZ.
THIS IS WHAT HAPPENS WHEN I WEAR A SKIRT FOR A CHANGE...
...

I'M THIRSTY!
HUH?! BUT YOU JUST FINISHED YOUR DRINK A SECOND AGO!
GO GET ME SOME-THING, WILL YOU?
YOU GOT THOSE COINS ON YOU, RIGHT?
...YOU'RE JUST TRYING TO MAKE ME FEEL LIKE I'M NOT *TOTALLY* USELESS, AREN'T YOU...
DON'T TRY TO BE SMART, STUPID! I THOUGHT YOU WANTED TO GRAB THOSE HEARTSTRINGS!!
YES-SIR!! I SURE DO, SIR!!
SO GO ON AND GET ME THAT DRINK!!
YESSIR!!

KA-TONK
...OH MY GOD...
ÔTANI IS SUCH A GREAT GUY.
I'M FALLING FOR HIM ALL OVER AGAIN.

WISH I COULD LOOK GOOD AND MAKE HIM FALL FOR ME ALL OVER AGAIN.
Right now I'm just a step-n-fetchit.
OH GOSH...
IS ÔTANI REALLY OKAY WITH THIS?
I'M NOT CUTE AND SWEET AND THOUGHTFUL LIKE HIS OLD GIRL-FRIEND.
I'M JUST THIS LAME, WORTH-LESS JUMBO-GAL.
DRINK&
IS HE REALLY FINE WITH HAVING ME BE HIS GIRL-FRIEND?

...OMI-
GOD.

THAT'S HIS EX-GIRLFRIEND, MAYU...

TOK
...HM?
I THOUGHT I JUST SAW...
HUH?
ENOUGH ALREADY!!
WHAT IS THIS?!
LIKE I'M NOT FREAKED OUT ENOUGH ABOUT HER, SHE HAS TO SHOW UP HERE?!

POPP
OWW-WWCH.
OH!
THERE YOU ARE!
WAAAAARGH!!
WHAT'S THE MATTER? ARE YOU OKAY?
ATSUSHI-KUN'S LOOKING FOR YOU.

OH. UM...
HEH, HEH...
OMI-GOSH!!
THAT MUST HURT SO MUCH!!
ARE THOSE BLISTERS?!
HUH?
YEAH...
GUESS THAT'S WHAT I GET FOR WEARING NEW SHOES.
OH, THERE'S A BENCH! SIT DOWN OVER THERE!!
HERE WE ARE.

FWIP
...YEAH. JUST LIKE I THOUGHT...
OF COURSE SHE HAS BAND-AIDS.
CAN YOU RAISE YOUR FOOT FOR A MINUTE?
SHE'S SO NICE TOO. AND SO PERFECT. AND SO OPPOSITE OF ME.
URR-RRGH...
HUH?!
DID THAT HURT?! ARE YOU OKAY?!

TOK
OH, THERE YOU ARE!
ATSUSHI-KUN!
WHAT? WHAT'S GOING ON HERE?
SHE HAD THESE BLISTERS ON HER FEET, AND THEY BURST...
HUH?
OH, YEAH, WOW! OUCH.
WHY DIDN'T YOU SAY ANY-THING?!
I CAN'T...
...TAKE THIS. I JUST CAN'T.
I LOOK SO STUPID RIGHT NOW.

YOU DON'T WANT TO GO OUT WITH SOMEONE THIS PATHETIC, DO YOU?
YOU'D RATHER GET BACK TOGETHER WITH MAYU, WOULDN'T YOU?
MRRF
MRRF
MRRF
COME TO THINK OF IT, SHE BROKE UP WITH HER BOYFRIEND. SO I GUESS IT'S...
...GOOD-BYE, ÔTANI...
I HAD A GREAT TIME WITH YOU, SHORT THOUGH IT WAS...
THANKS, MAYU.
I'LL TAKE OVER FROM HERE.
OH, REALLY? OKAY. SO...
OOPS, UM...
I'M SORRY, WHAT WAS YOUR NAME AGAIN?
HUH...?
KOIZUMI.

IT'S RISA KOIZUMI.
AND SHE'S MY GIRL-FRIEND.

...HUH?
OH.
YOU GUYS ARE GOING OUT?
YUP.
YOU BETTER GET GOING, MAYU. YOUR BOYFRIEND'S WAITING FOR YOU, RIGHT?
OH YEAH.
I BETTER GO.

I BUMPED INTO HER ON HER WAY BACK FROM THE BATHROOM.
SHE'S HERE WITH GIANT BABA. THEY GOT BACK TOGETHER.
SO THAT'S COOL. I WAS GLAD TO HEAR IT.
HE SAID "MY GIRL-FRIEND"...
...ARE YOU SURE ...?
HUH?
YOU SURE YOU WANT ME TO BE YOUR GIRLFRIEND...?
...NOW YOU ASK ME? JEEZ.

HERE, SHOW ME YOUR FOOT.
WHAT'D YOU HAVE TO WEAR THESE SHOES FOR? YOU SHOULD'VE JUST WORN WHAT YOU ALWAYS WEAR.
WELL, GOSH...
THIS WAS OUR FIRST DATE! I WANTED TO DRESS UP A LITTLE AND LOOK PRETTY...
HIS GIRL-FRIEND...
OOH.

THAT KINDA GOT ME. FELT A LITTLE TUG OVER HERE.
HUH? WHAT DID YOU SAY?
NOTHING.
I GUESS HE *IS* OKAY WITH HAVING ME BE HIS GIRL-FRIEND.

ÔTANI AND I...

RISA KOIZUMI (18)

5′8″

ATSUSHI ÔTANI (17)

5′2″

...HAVE BEEN KNOWN AS "ALL HANSHIN-KYOJIN" FROM THE VERY FIRST DAY OF HIGH SCHOOL.

BUT NOW...

IDIOT

STUPID

...WE'RE BOY-FRIEND-GIRL-FRIEND!

JUMBO-GAL

MICRO-BOY

NO WAAAAAY?!
SINCE WHEN?
WHY DIDN'T YOU TELL US?!
CONGRATULATIONS!!
HOW'D IT HAPPEN?
HUH?
I'M SO GLAD FOR YOU!!
OH.
YOU GUYS!
I DON'T BELIEVE THIS!
THAT'S GREAT.
YAARGH...
What do we do?
WHATEVER. YOU DEAL WITH IT.
ÔTANI! WAIT A SEC...
GWIP

CHAPTER 30

WE NEED TO TALK, GIRLFRIEND. GET YOUR BUTT OVER HERE AND GIVE US THE BLOW-BY-BLOW RIGHT NOW, OR ELSE.
Start-of-term Ceremony
IT'S THE START OF A NEW SEMESTER.
SO MUCH HAPPENED OVER SUMMER VACATION...
...THAT IT WENT BY IN A FLASH AND LASTED FOREVER, BOTH AT THE SAME TIME.
Ah ha ha
BUT THE UPSHOT IS, I AM A VERY HAPPY GIRL RIGHT NOW. ♡
I AM SO SURE, RISA! I MEAN, JEEZ!!

HOW COULD YOU STAY MUM ABOUT SOMETHING THIS BIG?!
HEE HEE...
I JUST CAN'T BELIEVE THIS...
AFTER ALL THE SUPPORT I GAVE YOU... AFTER ALL THE HAND-HOLDING AND PEP-TALKING...
...YOU DON'T EVEN CALL ME WHEN YOU FINALLY GET TOGETHER?
AND I THOUGHT WE WERE BEST FRIENDS...
URRRGH
I'M SORRY, NOBU!!
IT'S JUST THAT... I COULDN'T REALLY BELIEVE IT MYSELF. YOU KNOW?
RISA...
BUT NOW YOU CAN, RIGHT?

SHE'S MY GIRL-FRIEND.
YUP! ♡
GRIN
OH, FINE, I'LL FORGIVE YOU.
AND HEY, CONGRATULATIONS. IT'S PRETTY GREAT NEWS.
YEAH, RISA! IT *IS* GREAT NEWS.
HEH HEH HEH. THANK YOU...
SO, WOW.
OUR TALL-AND-SHORT COMEDY DUO HAS FINALLY BECOME BOYFRIEND-GIRLFRIEND.
SO TOUCHING...
This time for real.
THE "TALL-AND-SHORT" PART HASN'T CHANGED, THOUGH.
WELL, NOTHING YOU CAN DO ABOUT *THAT.*
HEY!

FTAP
FTAP
KOIZUMI SENPAI! NOBU SENPAI! ♡
HEY, SEIKO-CHAN! HOW'VE YOU BEEN?
I thought you were a giant flying squirrel for a sec.
I'VE BEEN FINE! HOW ARE YOU?
?
LISTEN TO THIS, SEIKO-CHAN!
RISA AND ÔTANI FINALLY GOT TOGETHER!
THEY DIIIIID?! OH MY GOD!!
OMIGOSH, SENPAI! YOU WORKED SO HARD FOR THIS, DIDN'T YOU?!
YEAH, WELL...
IT SURE TOOK LONG ENOUGH, HUH?
HEH HEH.

PLIP
PLIP
PLIP
OHHH! WOWWWW! HOW WONDERFUL, SENPAI!
I HOPE YOU'LL BE REALLY HAPPY TOGETHER!
MLURF
SEIKO-CHAN...
THANK YOU!! THANK YOU SO MUCH, SEIKO-CHAN!!
SKWEEZ
C'MON, LET'S GO, THE CEREMONY'S ABOUT TO START.
SNIF
I'M SO EXCITED FOR YOU, SENPAI!
THIS IS THE MOST THRILLING THING I'VE HEARD IN A LONG TIME!
IT'LL BE TOUGH GOING ...
...FOR ALL OF YOU THIRD-YEAR STUDENTS, BUT...
I REALLY DID WORK HARD FOR THIS. BUT IT WAS WORTH IT.
I'M SO GLAD I DIDN'T GIVE UP WHEN HE REJECTED ME.

NOW I CAN FINALLY...

...TELL THE WHOLE WORLD THAT ÔTANI'S MY BOY-FRIEND.

WHAT'RE YOU SO MAD ABOUT?

...

...I TOLD YOU NOT TO GO AROUND BLABBING IT TO EVERYBODY.
WHAT'S WRONG WITH THAT? THEY WERE GOING TO FIND OUT ANYWAY.
...
AWW, HOW CUUTE. HE'S EMBAR-RASSED!
DON'T BE SUCH A BAD SPORT, LOVER-BOY!

LEAVE ME ALONE, BONE-HEADS!!
WHAM
RISA!!
HARUKA...
I JUST HEARD FROM SEIKO!!
STOMP
STOMP
STOMP
IS IT REALLY TRUE THAT YOU'RE GOING OUT WITH THIS MIDGET?!
OH.
YES!

JABBER
OMIGOD! FOR REAL?!
YOU'RE GOING OUT?!
FINALLY!
GOSH, YOU GUYS! CONGRATULATIONS!
WOO-HOO! ALL RIGHT!!
WHAT THE...
HEH HEH HEH. THANK YOU...
WHAT'RE YOU THANKING THEM FOR? JEEZ!
WHY NOT? THEY WERE CONGRATULATING US.
And clapping, even.
BUT RISA–WHY?!
RISA! I'M SERIOUS! HOW COME?!
I MEAN, MY GOD, THIS IS A MINIATURE DACHSHUND, NOT A BOYFRIEND!!
SHAKE SHAKE
HUH?
WHO'RE YOU CALLING A DACHSHUND?!
WELL, YOU'RE TALKING SOME PRETTY RUDE STUFF ABOUT ME!!
YOU JUST SHUT UP AND BUTT OUT, SHRIMPY!! NOBODY'S TALKING TO YOU!!
And stop pointing at me!

NNGH
KTHUNK
Whoa.
OH FINE...
I KNEW A DAY LIKE THIS WOULD COME, SOONER OR LATER...
I KNEW IT ALL ALONG ...
OHHHH.
Ohhhhh!
POOOOR HARUKAAAA! DON'T CRY!
Boo hoo hoo, poor poor me...
THAT'S RIGHT, FEEL SORRY FOR ME. FEEL EVEN SORRIER FOR ME!
WHERE'D *THEY* ALL COME FROM?
RISA! HEY, RISA.
MR. NAKANO SAID FOR YOU AND ŌTANI-KUN TO GO SEE HIM LATER IN THE FACULTY ROOM.
HEH?

HE SAID YOU WERE THE ONLY ONES WHO NEVER TURNED IN YOUR FINAL SUMMER SCHOOL ASSIGNMENT.
Did you?
ASSIGN...
...MENT?
Seven times!! Do it seven times!!
Ohhhhh!
YOU FORGOT.
YEAH...
YOU FORGOT.
YEAH...
KA-CHAK
BEEEE
DRRRRRR
DRRRRRR
YOU FORGOT ABOUT IT.
WE'RE SORRY!!
WE'RE REALLY SORRY!!
WELL, APOLOGIZING ISN'T GOING TO GET IT DONE.
I WANT IT ON MY DESK MONDAY MORNING.

GUESS ŌTANI ISN'T MY WHOLE LIFE, AFTER ALL. I HAVE OTHER STUFF TO THINK ABOUT...
MONDAY MORNING? THAT JUST GIVES US THE WEEKEND...
OH, MAN... I'M STARTING TO THINK WE MIGHT END UP HERE ANOTHER YEAR, FOR REAL.

HEY, LET'S SPLIT IT 50/50 AND DO IT TOGETHER.
That assignment.
WHERE? YOU WANNA GO TO THE LIBRARY WITH SUZUKI AND CHIHARU?

The library, ugh...I hate quiet places like that. They make me wanna scream.
I know, me too...

OKAY, SO...
YOU WANNA DO IT AT MY HOUSE?

IS THAT OKAY?!
YEAH, IT'S COOL.
mmmgh

REMEMBER THAT TIME YOU CAME OVER?

WELL, MY MOM FELL IN LOVE WITH YOU OR SOMETHING.

SHE'S BEEN, LIKE, BRING HER OVER, EVER SINCE.

ARE YOU SERIOUS?!

GUESS YOU'RE SO BIG, YOU MAKE A BIG IMPRESSION.

HEY! WHAT'S THAT MEAN?

I'LL COME PICK YOU UP AT THE STATION TOMORROW.

WOW! REALLY?!

I'M GOING OVER TO HIS HOUSE TO STUDY.

tweeet

chrp chrp chrp

THAT IS JUST SO... GIRL-FRIENDY!

...HEY.

 2

UFJ (the bank) and USJ (Universal Studios Japan)...

I still need to think a little before I say one or the other, or I get them mixed up.

USJ is pretty close to my house, so I've already been there five or six times. It's a really... fun place...! It's not so much the attractions as the people who come. They're all soaking wet, and yet they all have huge grins on their faces like they're big fools or something. I'm talking drenched. Wherever you go in that place, they're splashing water on you. But everyone's smiling. Isn't that great...? You don't find many places where you can see that many people laughing all at once. It's a balm for the soul. Keep smiling, everybody!

A laugh a day keeps the doctor away.

Gotta smile!

Would your mother be fond of sweets, I wonder?
HUH?
I purchased some cake as a little gift for her, you see.

I BELIEVE SHE IS FOND OF SWEETS, YES.

Oh, marvelous!

WHO THE HECK ARE YOU, ANYWAY?

Why do you inquire? Am I behaving unusually?

LIKE THERE'S ANYTHING *USUAL* ABOUT YOU TODAY?

ATCHAN!!
Hm?
MIMI.
WHAT'S UP?
GOT THE MUNCHIES. I'M GOING TO THE STORE TO GET SOMETHING.
SKREE
...ATCHAN ...?
MIMI...?
UH...
WHO MIGHT THIS BE...?
HM?

MY NEXT-DOOR NEIGHBOR.
OH.
WOOOH. OMIGOD, SHE'S A TOTAL KNOCK-OUT!
NICE TO MEETCHA!
I'M MIMI YOSHIOKA AND I'M A SECOND-YEAR MIDDLE SCHOOLER!
MIDDLE SCHOOLER?! GOSH, YOU LOOK SO GROWN-UP!
YOU THINK?
AND WHO'S THIS, ATCHAN?
A FRIEND FROM SCHOOL?
HUH?

PITTER
PATTER
...MY GIRL-FRIEND.
HEH HEH. HI! NICE TO MEET YOU TOO.
NO WAAAY!!
Eh?
SINCE WHEN?!
WELL, YEAH, 'CUZ I NEVER TOLD YOU.
I NEVER HEARD ABOUT THIS!!
YOU GOTTA TELL ME!!
HEY, KOIZUMI, GET BACK ON.
AYE AYE, SIR!

shooo
BYE, MIMI! I'LL SEE YOU AROUND!
BOY, WAS SHE PRETTY...
MM.
SHE MODELS FOR SOME GIRLS' MAGAZINE OR SOME-THING.
OMIGOD! WOW!! HOW COOL!
THAT'S RIGHT, SHE WAS REALLY TALL TOO!
ABOUT THE SAME HEIGHT AS YOU, PROBABLY.
OOH, SO MAYBE I CAN BE A MODEL TOO...
qwa ha ha
With **that** face?
HEY! THAT'S WHAT YOU SAY TO YOUR GIRL-FRIEND?!
worgh
WILL YOU SIT STILL?!

OOOH!! COME IN, COME IN!!
HOW NICE TO SEE YOU AGAIN!!
HELLO, MRS. ŌTANI!
HOW'VE YOU BEEN? I'VE BEEN WAITING FOR YOU TO COME OVER AGAIN!
YOU HAVE, REALLY?! MY GOSH, I'M SO GLAD TO HEAR THAT!
SO COME ON, YOU CAN TELL ME! YOU AND ATCHAN ARE GOING OUT, AREN'T YOU?
hee hee
WELL, YES...
I JUST KNEW IT!
THIS SON OF MINE... YOU KNOW THE LAST TIME YOU CAME OVER? HE KEPT SAYING YOU WEREN'T HIS GIRLFRIEND!
WHAT'S HE GOT TO HIDE IT FOR, I'D LIKE TO KNOW?
ALL RIGHT, MOM, NOW JUST GET THE HECK OUTTA HERE!!
YOU WANT TO SEE PICTURES OF ATCHAN WHEN HE WAS LITTLE?
DEFI-NITELY!!
YAAAAY
MOM! YOU DEAF OR SOME-THING?!
indergarten
OOH.

ISN'T HE A CUTIE?
THAT IS SOOOO CUUUUTE! ♡
ALBUM
FLIT
WHY'D YOU HAVE TO BRING THAT OUT?! JEEZ! YOU ARE DUST, MOM!!
PHLAP
HEY, ISN'T THIS THAT GIRL MIMI WE JUST MET OUTSIDE?
HUH?
OH, YEAH...
GOSH, PRETTY GIRLS ARE PRETTY FROM THE TIME THEY'RE LITTLE, HUH?
ZWUP
TAKE A LOOK AT ATCHAN IN THIS PICTURE, HE'S...
HM?
SHE'S HERE SO WE CAN DO A HOMEWORK ASSIGNMENT, OKAY?! NOW GET OUT, 'CUZ YOU'RE IN OUR WAY!!
ALL RIGHT, ALL RIGHT, I'M GOING.
KA-CHAK
DON'T WANT TO BE IN YOUR WAY WHEN YOU'RE... DOING HOMEWORK, DID YOU SAY?
Ha!
HEH?
WILL YOU SHUT UP AND GET OUT?!

...
...
RUSTLE
SO WHAT, YOU CAN TALK TO MY MOM AND NOT TO ME?!
HUUH?!
WELL, GOSH. I MEAN...
...WHEN IT'S SUDDENLY JUST THE TWO OF US, ALONE, I'M FEELING KINDA NERVOUS.
SO WHAT'S THE DEAL, WE HAVE TO DO ALL OF THESE QUESTIONS FOR THAT ASSIGNMENT?

YEAH.
HOLY COW, THAT'S A LOT...
FLIP
...IT FEELS LIKE...
...I'M SEEING ÔTANI'S ROOM FOR THE FIRST TIME.
THE LAST TIME I WAS HERE...
...I WAS SO DESPERATE TO GET HIS ATTENTION, I HARDLY LOOKED AROUND.
WE'RE ALL ALONE IN MY BED-ROOM...
...AND I'M NOT FEELING ANY URGE TO MAKE ANY KINDA MOVE ON YOU.
BUT THIS TIME...
...IT'S DIFFERENT.

THIS TIME, I'M HIS GIRL-FRIEND.
AND ÔTANI'S MY BOY-FRIEND.
WE'RE GOING OUT...
SHWA
...
HEY, ÔTANI ...?
IS MIMI YOUR NEIGH-BOR ON THAT SIDE?
HUH? YEAH.

HOW COME?
WAS SHE WATCHING US...?
HEY.
YOU GROW UP WITH A GORGEOUS GIRL LIKE THAT NEXT DOOR, DIDN'T ANYTHING EVER HAPPEN?
WHADDAYA MEAN, HAPPEN?
OH, JUST ASKING ...
OR DID I JUST IMAGINE THAT?
WELL, LIKE GETTING A CRUSH ON HER, OR...
AS IF. GIMME A BREAK.
REALLY?
LOOK, IT'S JUST LIKE YOU AND THAT DOPE HARUKA OF YOURS.
YOU KNOW EACH OTHER SINCE YOU'RE LITTLE, NOTHING'S GONNA HAPPEN.
OHHH... YEAH, THAT'S TRUE.
PLUS, MIMI'S BEEN WAY TALLER THAN ME SINCE DAY ONE.

WELL, *I'M* WAY TALLER THAN YOU.
...OH. YEAH.
WELL, WITH YOU, IT DOESN'T BOTHER ME.

...OH, REALLY.
SMAK
IS THAT SO!
ARGH!
SMAK
OWW...!
WHAT?! CUT IT OUT, IT HURTS!!
SMAK
HEE HEE HEE HEE HEE! OH, REALLY?!
IT'S LIKE HE WAS SAYING...
...THAT I'M DIFFERENT. THAT I'M SPECIAL.
SMAK

HEE HEE HEE HEE!

I *SAID,* CUT IT OUT! THAT REALLY HURTS!!

FFF
HEH HEH!
...
WHY...
DO YOU ALWAYS HAVE TO START LAUGHING?!
ARRRGH!
I'M SORRY, BUT I JUST CAN'T TAKE THE TENSION!!
TAKE IT!!
ZING
...

...AFTER ALL THIS TIME...
...I GOT TO BE ÔTANI'S SPECIAL GIRL. I FINALLY DID...
ATCHAAAAAAN!!
GWUMF
WH AM
GWUMF
GWUMF
OOPS!

DID I INTERRUPT SOMETHING?
Ha ha ha ha ha.
Nah. Not really.
WHATCHA COME BUSTIN' IN HERE FOR, ANYWAY?
RUSTLE
I BROUGHT YOU YOUR DAILY BOTTLE OF MILK! ♪

DAILY...
...BOTTLE OF MILK?
SHE BRINGS ME MILK EVERY DAY, SAYING IT'S GONNA HELP ME GROW.
TODAY'S MILK IS EXTRA-SPECIAL, ATCHAN! IT'S FLOWN IN EVERY MORNING STRAIGHT FROM HOKKAIDO, AND IT'S CHOCK-FULL OF CALCIUM!
THAT'S WHY I BROUGHT IT STRAIGHT OVER, 'CUZ IT'S SO FRESH!

HEE HEE HEE HEE HEE HEE!
WHAT'S SO DARN FUNNY?!
SHE BRINGS YOU MILK? EVERY DAY?!
HEY! ATCHAN, I JUST HEARD YOUR MOM CALLING YOU.

SO WHAT, I GO DOWNSTAIRS AND YOU STAY HERE? I DON'T THINK SO.
BUT I WANNA GET TO KNOW YOUR GIRL-FRIEND! JUST FOR A WHILE, PLEEZE?
NO! SHE'S OVER HERE TO DO HOME-WORK, OKAY? WE GOTTA STUDY!
OH COME ON, ÔTANI. JUST FOR A LITTLE WHILE.
YAAAY!
...
JUST FOR A LITTLE WHILE!
I WON'T STAY LONG!
KLIK
TEE HEE!
TEE HEE!

BOY, IS SHE CUTE... ♡
SO I HEARD YOU'RE A MODEL?
YUP!
HOW TALL ARE YOU?
FIVE FOOT EIGHT!
OMIGOD! THAT'S THE SAME AS ME!
OH, SO WE'RE THE SAME HEIGHT.
BUT ATCHAN SAYS HE DOESN'T LIKE GIRLS WHO'RE TALLER THAN HIM!
OH... YEAH, I KNOW.
BUT...
WITH YOU, IT DOESN'T BOTHER ME.
MY HEIGHT DOESN'T BOTHER HIM, HE SAID.
FOR SOME REASON!
Heh heh.
...

OH REALLY?! WOW!
HEY, DID YOU KNOW THAT HIS OLD GIRL-FRIEND WAS REALLY SMALL?
YEAH, I KNOW HER...
AND SHE *IS* REALLY SMALL AND CUTE...
THAT'S WHY I DECIDED TO GIVE UP ON ATCHAN, MYSELF.
WHAT...?
YOU HAVE A CRUSH ON ÔTANI, MIMI?
YUP!
BUT ATCHAN ONLY LIKES SHORT GIRLS, AND I'M REALLY TALL, RIGHT?
SO, SINCE I CAN'T SHRINK, MY ONLY HOPE IS FOR ATCHAN TO GROW TALLER THAN ME.
CHIK
AND THAT'S WHY I BRING HIM A BOTTLE OF MILK EVERY DAY.

CHIK
CHIK
...
CHIK
OH... UH-HUH...
KLAK
CHIK
AND THEN, WHEN ATCHAN GREW TALLER THAN ME...
...I WAS GOING TO BE HIS GIRLFRIEND. THAT WAS THE PLAN, ANYWAY.
OH... GOSH... SHE'S TOTALLY CRAZY ABOUT HIM...
I FEEL KINDA BAD... SORRY.
UMM... WELL, GOSH...

GYAAAAARGH!
Tch!
DARN, I MISSED.
YOU FEEL KINDA BAD...? YOU'RE SORRY?
"MY HEIGHT DOESN'T BOTHER HIM, FOR SOME REASON." HAH! YOU THINK YOU'RE REALLY SPECIAL, DON'T YOU?
WANT ME TO PASS A WET NOODLE THROUGH YOUR NOSE AND TIE IT IN A BOW, YOU STUPID COW?

Whaa-aaa...?
No thank you, I'll pass.
WHAT STINKING LIES DID YOU TELL TO BLACKMAIL ATCHAN INTO DATING YOU, HUH? I'M SO ONTO YOU, SCUM!
I...
THERE IS NO WAY ATCHAN WOULD EVER ASK A BIMBO LIKE YOU OUT, THAT MUCH I KNOW FOR SURE. NO WAY!
Um...
Mimi...
DON'T YOU EVER SAY MY NAME WITH THAT DISGUSTING MOUTH OF YOURS, OR I'LL STAB YOU!!
With this pencil!!
YOU SPEND EVEN ONE MORE DAY AROUND ATCHAN...
...AND I'LL MAKE SURE YOU HATE LIFE, DOGFACE. BELIEVE IT.
OH MY GOD...
KA-CHAK

KREE
KLIK
MY MOM MADE US SOME TEA.
ÔTANI! HELP, SHE'S...
HEH?
SHE'S WHAT?
SWITCH
YAAAY! HE BROUGHT US CAKE! ♡

...HUH?
ACTUALLY, KOIZUMI BROUGHT US THIS CAKE.
OH, SHE DID? HOW NICE OF HER!
MMM, I WANT THAT CHOCO-LATE ONE!
CAN I HAVE IT?
UH...
WAIT A MINUTE ...
UH... SURE... GO RIGHT AHEAD...
Please...
YAAAAAY!
DID I IMAGINE THAT BEFORE ...?
MWUNCH
WHAT'S THE MATTER, KOIZUMI?

AREN'T YOU GONNA HAVE ANY?
UH... NAH...
SNEER
HEY, MIMI. WHEN YOU'RE DONE WITH THAT, YOU LEAVE!
OH-KAAY! ♡
NO, I DIDN'T IMAGINE THAT BEFORE...

WHAT DOES YOUR FAVORITE MODEL LOOK LIKE IN HER FREE TIME?
PEEK INTO MIMI'S CLOSET TO SEE WHAT SHE'S WEARING THIS FALL!

Mimi's
private fashion

MIMI YOSHIOKA (13)

These are Mimi's top picks for the cold weather around the corner!

CHAPTER 31

HMMM-MMM...
Hi, Risa!
WHAT'RE YOU DOING WITH THAT?
I MEAN, LIKE, SINCE WHEN DO YOU CHECK OUT GIRLY FASHION MAGS?
Peach
THIS GIRL WHO LIVES NEXT DOOR TO ÔTANI IS A MODEL IN THIS ONE.
Here, see? Her.
OMIGOD, FOR REAL?! LET'S SEE, WHERE? WOW, SHE'S REALLY PRETTY!
SHE LOOKS KINDA EVIL, THOUGH.
YOU REALLY THINK SO?
I DON'T KNOW IF SHE *IS*. BUT SHE SURE *LOOKS* LIKE IT.
YOU MEET HER?
WELL, YEAH... AND THE THING IS, SEE...
HEY.

THAT'S MIMI.
HI, ŌTANI.
HI, ŌTANI...
HEY...
HAVE YOU SEEN HER SINCE? HAS SHE SAID ANYTHING TO YOU ABOUT ME?
HM? OH YEAH. SHE SEEMS TO LIKE YOU A WHOLE LOT.
SAID SHE WANTS TO HANG OUT WITH YOU AGAIN.
WHAT?
WHAT?
...
YOU SPEND EVEN ONE MORE DAY AROUND ATCHAN...
...AND I'LL MAKE SURE YOU HATE LIFE, DOGFACE. BELIEVE IT.

UH, NOTHING. FORGET IT...
...
NO USE TELLING ÔTANI ABOUT THAT, I GUESS. I MEAN, HE'D NEVER BELIEVE ME.
bzzzzzzz
?
Okay. EVERYBODY SIT DOWN, PLEASE.
WONDER IF SHE REALLY MEANT IT.
WELL, HOW AM I SUPPOSED TO *NOT* SPEND ANOTHER DAY AROUND HIM...
...WHEN I'M IN THE SAME CLASS AS HIM, NOT TO MENTION HIS GIRLFRIEND?
ATCHAN!♡
KREEP

SHALL WE GO TURN IN THAT SUMMER SCHOOL ASSIGNMENT? ♡
tee hee
DON'T CALL ME "ATCHAN," IT CREEPS ME OUT!!
WHY SHOULD IT CREEP YOU OUT?! I'M YOUR GIRLFRIEND!
IT JUST DOES!! I MEAN, *JEEZ!!* YOU WANT *ME* TO SUDDENLY START CALLING YOU "RISA-CHAN"?!
BLUSH
YOU WILL?
AS IF I'D EVER DO THAT! KOIZUMI!! WHAT'RE YOU BLUSHING FOR, YOU DOPE?!
PUSA
I'D LOVE IT IF YOU STARTED CALLING ME "RISA-CHAN."
OR EVEN JUST "RISA," ACTUALLY.
GET OUTTA HERE, LAME-BRAIN!
...

OH, WELL. I GUESS I SHOULDN'T FREAK OUT TOO MUCH ABOUT MIMI.
..Whaddaya mean, "lame-brain"?!
I mean "lame-brain," lame-brain!!
THOSE TWO ARE THE SAME NOW AS BEFORE.
WELL, IT'D BE WEIRD IF THEY SUDDENLY CHANGED.
Sorry it was late...
AFTER ALL, NO MATTER WHAT SHE SAYS OR DOES TO ME...
...SO LONG AS I'VE GOT ŌTANI'S LOVE, I AM A HAPPY GIRL. ♡
tee hee
GOSH, YOU DON'T HAVE TO GET SO MAD ABOUT IT.
I MEAN, YOU NEVER GET MAD WHEN MIMI CALLS YOU "ATCHAN." SO WHY LOSE IT IF I DO?
'CUZ *YOU* JUST CALL ME THAT TO MAKE FUN OF ME, THAT'S WHY!!
GO HOME BY YOURSELF, STUPID IDIOT!!
How can you say that?
THAT IS NOT EVEN TRUE, *ATCHAN.*
See?
YOU'RE *TOTALLY* MAKING FUN OF ME!!

ATCHAAAN!
YOU GOING HOME NOW?
WHAT THE...?
SPEAK OF THE DEVIL...
WHAT'RE YOU DOING HERE?
I THOUGHT WE COULD GO HOME TOGETHER. ♡
HUNH?
EH...?
I WANNA GET TO KNOW YOUR GIRLFRIEND BETTER! I WANNA FIND OUT EVERYTHING ABOUT HER. ♡
NOT A WHOLE LOT THERE TO FIND OUT.
GRRR

HEY! WHAT'S *THAT* SUPPOSED TO MEAN?!

HMPH

HEE HEE!

THAT WAS *SO* FUNNY!

OH...

HA HA...

OKAY OKAY, ENOUGH OF THAT. NOW GET OUTTA HERE, MIMI.

WHAAAT? HOW COME?

BECAUSE I DO NOT WANT TO GO HOME ***SURROUNDED*** BY TWO ***JUMBO-GALS!!***

HA HA HA HA HA! 'CUZ YOU'LL TURN INTO THE CAPTURED SPACE ALIEN, RIGHT?

SHUT UP!!

Who knows, maybe you'll hear messages from outer space!
You'll hear a message from outer space if you say that again!
I'M GOING AHEAD!!
WAIT! HANG ON, ŌTANI...
HEY, DINGBAT.
GET YOUR BIG BUTT OVER HERE.

blah
blah
blah

WARGH ...
HMMMM
SHE'S TOTALLY STARING AT ME...

WHAT'S SHE GOING TO SAY TO ME THIS TIME...?
UH...

SO, UMMM...
WHAT DID YOU WANT TO SEE ME ABOUT...?
I DON'T GET IT.
HUH?

ARE YOU REALLY ATCHAN'S GIRLFRIEND? OR WAS HE JUST KIDDING WHEN HE SAID THAT?

I'M REALLY HIS GIRL-FRIEND.
hee hee
...
I DON'T GET IT.
I MEAN, HOW COME? WHAT'D YOU DO?
WHAT'D I DO...? WELL, BASI-CALLY...
I WENT FOR IT.
I WORKED REALLY, REALLY HARD TO GET HERE!
BIG HONKING DEAL! *I'M* GOING FOR IT! I'M WORKING REALLY, REALLY HARD TOO, STUPID!!
YOU'VE *SEEN* HOW SWEET I AM AROUND HIM! COME ON, ADMIT IT, I'M REALLY SWEET AROUND HIM, AREN'T I?!
I'VE BEEN ACTING LIKE THAT AROUND HIM SINCE DAY ONE, OKAY?! HE THINKS THAT'S WHAT I'M LIKE ALL THE TIME, OKAY?! YOU GOT ANY IDEA HOW *HARD* THAT IS?!
Oh, uh, yeah.

I CAN IMAGINE ...
That would be really hard.
Wow...
That must be really tough.
AND THAT ISN'T ALL, EITHER.
THAT MILK I BUY HIM EVERY DAY TO MAKE HIM GROW TALLER, IT ADDS UP. COSTS ME A LOTTA MONEY, OKAY?
AND IT'S NOT EVEN WORKING. ATCHAN HASN'T GROWN DIDDLY SQUAT SINCE, LIKE, HIS FIRST YEAR OF MIDDLE SCHOOL.
ARE YOU SERIOUS ?!
That long?!
I'M SERIOUS.
MEANWHILE, I KEEP GROWING ENOUGH FOR BOTH OF US, I SWEAR.
I WAS ALREADY FIVE FOOT SEVEN BY THE END OF SIXTH GRADE, IF YOU CAN BELIEVE IT.
I CAN.
'CUZ I WAS A LITTLE OVER FIVE FOOT SIX WHEN I WAS IN ELEMENTARY SCHOOL!
NO WAY, FOR REAL?!
TOTALLY FOR REAL. I'VE BEEN THE TALLEST KID IN MY CLASS EVERY YEAR SINCE KINDER-GARTEN.
ME TOO!
I WAS ALWAYS TALLER THAN THE TALLEST BOY, EVERY YEAR!

③

Speaking of sopping wet...

My house has a water sprite that gets everything wet...

Well, actually she's my mom...

She comes into my room holding the mail, it's drenched and wrinkled... You give her a magazine, it gets drenched and wrinkled...You show her a photograph, it gets drenched and wrinkled...

So okay, she's always doing some household chore or other that involves water, which is fine, but could she please wipe her hands off before holding things! When I tell her that, she feels bad and promises to mend her ways. So then I think it's okay, but when she walks into my room waving a postcard that just arrived in the mail for me, sure enough, it's drenched and wrinkled...

Your hands, Mom. Wipe them, please.

"PLEASE. WIPE. YOUR. HANDS."

Do you understand?

Hamburgers in my house are served on sopping wet plates.

I live in Waterworld!

YUP YUP YUP, ME TOO!
DIDN'T YOU *HATE* THAT? YOU TOTALLY STICK OUT LIKE A SORE THUMB, DON'T YOU!
YEAH, LIKE, YOU SAY TWO WORDS AND THE TEACHER'S ON YOUR CASE, WHEN EVERYBODY ELSE IS TALKING A LOT MORE.

BUT HEY! I DIDN'T COME HERE TO START THIS BUDDY-BUDDY SUPPORT GROUP WITH YOU, YOU STUPID WARTHOG!!
UH-HUH? ARE YOU DOING NORI-TSUKKOMI?
SHUT YER YAP, BUTT-HEAD!!

WHO CARES HOW TALL *YOU* WERE, ANYWAY?! THE POINT IS...

...ALL MY LIFE, I'VE BEEN BUSTING MY BUTT TO GET ATCHAN TO FALL FOR ME.
BUT THEN HE STARTED GOING OUT WITH THAT TINY GIRL, SO I GAVE UP 'CUZ I KNEW I DIDN'T STAND A CHANCE WITH HIM AFTER ALL.

YOU MEAN THAT GIRL MAYU, RIGHT? KANZAKI-SAN? YEAH, SHE'S SUPER-CUTE, ISN'T SHE?
YOU SEE HER AND YOU THINK, IF THAT'S HIS TYPE, HE'LL NEVER FALL FOR SOMEONE MY HEIGHT IN A MILLION YEARS. I KNOW, I KNOW!
EXACTLY. AND ON TOP OF BEING SHORT AND CUTE, SHE TURNS OUT TO BE REALLY NICE, LIKE, FOR REAL. I THOUGHT SHE MIGHT BE NASTY UNDER-NEATH, BUT...
OH YEAH, YOU MEAN LIKE YOUR-SELF?
EXACTLY, SINCE I'M A TOTAL WITCH MYSELF...
HEY, WHO ASKED YOU TO BUTT IN, ANYHOW?! JUST SHUT UP AND LISTEN, BIGMOUTH!!
OH, PARDON ME.
YOU JUST MADE ME CALL MYSELF A TOTAL WITCH!!
SO THEN, WHEN HE FINALLY BREAKS UP WITH HER AFTER THE LONGEST TIME, HIS NEXT GIRL-FRIEND IS *YOU?!*
YOU'RE *BIG,* YOU'RE *STUPID* ...!!
I'M LIKE, WHAT *IS* THIS?!
URGH.
LISTEN.
I JUST KNOW THERE IS NO WAY I WOULD EVER LOSE TO *YOU.*

ATCHAN'S MINE, AND I'M GONNA TAKE HIM AWAY FROM YOU. NO MATTER WHAT!
THAT'S ALL, DOG-FACE.
KTUNK
LATER.
Huh?
...
W-WAIT, MIMI-CHAN!

...WHAT?

...I...

I'M SORRY, BUT COULD YOU LEND ME SOME MONEY...?

WHAT?!

I ONLY HAVE FIFTY YEN ON ME...

50 YEN IS ABOUT 43 CENTS

FIFTY YEN?!

YOU CAME IN HERE WITH JUST FIFTY YEN ON YOU?!

WHAT ARE YOU, RETARDED?!

NO, IT'S JUST THAT I FORGOT... I BOUGHT THIS MAGAZINE THIS MORNING, SO...

A *MAGAZINE?!*

YEAH! THIS ONE! THAT *YOU'RE* IN, MIMI-CHAN!

YOU WERE SO PRETTY I COULDN'T RESIST BUYING IT, EVEN THOUGH IT MEANT SPENDING ALL THE MONEY I HAD ON ME.

SHWA

Peach

...

OHH, REALLYY ...?

WELL, OKAY, I'LL LEND YOU SOME CASH THEN. JUST THIS ONCE.

THANK YOU SO MUCH! YOU ARE SOOO NICE. ♡

RUMMAGE
RUMMAGE
TURNS OUT I LEFT MY WALLET AT SCHOOL! *NOW* WHAT DO WE DO?!
YOU WHAAAT?!
...Shall we... make a run for it...?
...
SHWAP
...

THAT'LL BE 630 YEN, PLEASE.
HERE...
PHEW... THANK GOOD-NESS.
SORRY, ŌTANI. I'M REALLY SORRY ABOUT THAT.
I'M REALLY SORRY, ATCHAN.
WELL, WELL. THANK YOU VERY MUCH.
I'LL BRING YOU FIVE CARTONS OF MILK TOMORROW TO MAKE UP FOR IT.
NO BIGGIE, I LOVE BEING CALLED OUT TO PAY PEOPLE'S BILLS.
HEY, YOU SOUNDED TOTALLY UNTHRILLED!
I'M VERY THRILLED.

Have you grown lately?

Haven't measured so I don't know.

...

IT REALLY IS LIKE SHE'S A COMPLETELY DIFFERENT PERSON.

I COULD NEVER PULL THAT OFF.

WELL, YOU GO ON HOME, MIMI. I'LL SEE YOU LATER.
HUH? HOW COME?!
I'M GONNA TAKE KOIZUMI HOME FIRST, SO.

HEY!!
YUMP
...OH REALLY ...?
!
I'LL BE FINE, ŌTANI!
I CAN GO HOME BY MYSELF!
WHAT FOR? HOP ON, I'LL GIVE YOU A RIDE.
NO, REALLY, UM...!
...ATCHAN.
HMM?

WHY'RE YOU GOING OUT WITH HER? WHAT DO YOU *LIKE* ABOUT HER?

EH?

HUH ?!

WHERE THE HECK DID *THAT* COME...

WELL, GOSH! SHE'S SO COMPLETELY DIFFERENT FROM YOUR OLD GIRL-FRIEND.

PLUS, SHE'S WAY TALLER THAN YOU.

AND SHE WALTZES INTO COFFEE SHOPS WITH JUST FIFTY YEN ON HER.

I JUST DON'T GET WHAT YOU SEE IN HER, THAT'S ALL.

...WELL, JEEZ.

WHO CARES WHAT I SEE IN HER, ANYWAY?

WHADDAYA MEAN, WHO CARES?!

IT'S NOT EXACTLY THE KIND OF THING YOU MAKE PUBLIC ANNOUNCE-MENTS ABOUT, OKAY?!

BUT I WANNA KNOW.

COME ON, ATCHAN. ANNOUNCE IT!

NO!

FORGET ABOUT IT, MIMI. IT'S GOT NOTHING TO DO WITH YOU, ANYWAY.

YES IT DOES ***SO*** HAVE SOME-THING TO DO WITH ME!!

BECAUSE I LOVE YOU A THOUSAND TIMES MORE THAN SHE DOES, ATCHAN!!
...MIMI ...

HUH?
WAS THAT FOR REAL?!
...
UM...

UH... MIMI-CHAN...
YOU ARE SO STUPID, ATCHAN!!
DASH
MIMI!!
AAA-ARGH...
...HOLY COW. THAT REALLY FREAKED ME OUT.
WHAT HAPPENED TO HER?
...
...YOU NEVER NOTICED HOW SHE FELT ABOUT YOU BEFORE THIS?
HUH?

YOU KNEW SHE HAD THE HOTS FOR ME, KOIZUMI?
OH, FOR CRYING OUT LOUD...I KNOW HOW MIMI'S FEELING RIGHT NOW SO WELL IT *HURTS.* I MEAN, *JEEZ!*

OH YEAH? AND HOW'S THAT?

SHE'S BANGING HER HEAD AGAINST THE WALL IN DISBELIEF AT HOW TOTALLY *CLUELESS* YOU ARE.
...

WELL, *JEEZ!!*

WHO WANTS TO BE SO FULL OF HIM-SELF THAT HE GOES AROUND THINKING "OH, SHE'S HOT FOR ME" ABOUT PRACTICALLY EVERY GIRL HE KNOWS?!

IT'S NOT ABOUT BEING FULL OF YOUR-SELF, IT'S ABOUT NOTICING PEOPLE'S FEEL-INGS!!

SHE'S BEEN TRYING REALLY HARD TO MAKE YOU LIKE HER, OKAY? SO THE LEAST YOU CAN DO IS NOTICE THAT.

...
ARR-RRGH...
SO WHAT'RE YOU GONNA DO?
ABOUT WHAT...?
ABOUT MIMI!
WELL, WHAT *CAN* I DO...?
I MEAN, COME ON...
YOU KNOW WHAT SHE TOLD ME AT THE COFFEE SHOP? THAT SHE WAS GONNA TAKE YOU AWAY FROM ME, NO MATTER WHAT.
WHAAAT?!
SO WHAT AM I GONNA DO IF SHE SUCCEEDS?

GIMME A BREAK.

...

...WELL, GOSH. TELL YOU THE TRUTH, I DON'T GET IT EITHER.

GET WHAT?

YOU KNOW, WHAT MIMI WAS TALKING ABOUT EARLIER.

WHY'RE YOU GOING OUT WITH HER?

I JUST DON'T GET WHAT YOU SEE IN HER.

I'M BIG, I'M STUPID, I'M NOT GOOD FOR ANYTHING... SO WHY'RE YOU GOING OUT WITH ME?

I DON'T REALLY GET WHAT YOU SEE IN ME EITHER.

AND THAT'S WHY...

...IT KINDA SCARES ME WHEN A TOTALLY BEAUTIFUL GIRL LIKE MIMI...

...SAYS SHE'S GOING TO GO ALL OUT TO TAKE YOU AWAY FROM ME.

...WELL, SORRY, BUT...
I CAN'T TELL YOU, 'CUZ I DON'T KNOW WHY I'M GOING OUT WITH YOU EITHER.

YOU DON'T KNOW ...?

NOPE. NOT A CLUE.

WONDER WHY...?

IT *JUST HAPPENED?*

OR MAYBE IT'S WHAT THEY CALL "TEMPORARY INSANITY"?

HEY! WAIT A MINUTE!!

"THAT'S RIGHT, YOUR HONOR, WHEN I CAME TO MY SENSES, WE WERE GOING OUT..."

ÔTANI!!

FINE!! FORGET IT!! I'M NEVER ASKING YOU AGAIN!!
HEY, I WAS JUST KIDDING. C'MON, GET ON THE BACK.
YOU *BETTER* BE KIDDING!! I WOULD *THROTTLE* YOU IF YOU WERE SERIOUS!!
...STILL, THOUGH ...
...I REALLY DO WONDER WHAT HE LIKES ABOUT ME.

AND EVEN THOUGH WE'RE GOING OUT NOW...
...IT'S NOT LIKE HE'S ALL OVER ME ALL THE TIME, OR LIKE HE EVER TELLS ME HE LOVES ME OR ANYTHING.
WELL, IT WOULD BE KINDA FREAKY IF HE DID.
BUT THEN HOW DO I KNOW HOW HE FEELS ABOUT ME? I SWEAR, I'M JUST AS INSECURE AROUND HIM NOW AS I WAS BEFORE WE STARTED GOING OUT.
THAT KINDA TICKS ME OFF!!
ZWING
HEY! STOP THAT!
Don't swing your legs.
...BASICALLY...

I WANT TO BE ONE HUNDRED PERCENT POSITIVE THAT HE DEFINITELY LOVES ME FOR SURE...
Like what, you want him to jump off a building for you or something?!
Wh-wh-wh-what's the matter, Risa? Are you okay?!
HAAAAGH...
WHAT IS IT? DID SOMETHING HAPPEN?
YOU KNOW THAT MODEL GIRL WHO LIVES NEXT DOOR TO HIM? SHE TOLD ŌTANI SHE LOVES HIM.
WHAAAAT?!
SO WHAT DID HE DO?!
I DON'T KNOW...
OH.

ÔTANI!
YO.

WHAT HAPPENED WITH MIMI AFTER THAT?
DID YOU SEE HER?
NOPE.
I KEEP GOING OVER THERE, BUT SHE WON'T COME OUT OF HER ROOM.

WAS THAT FOR REAL?

...I GUESS IT WAS A HUGE SHOCK FOR HER TO SEE THAT STUPID LOOK ON HIS FACE AND REALIZE HE'D NEVER THOUGHT ABOUT HER THAT WAY AT ALL...

SHE WON'T COME OUT OF HER ROOM?
OMIGOD, MIMI, I KNOW! I KNOW WHAT THAT'S LIKE!!
ÔTANI IS SUCH A KNUCKLE-HEAD!!
YOU PICKING A FIGHT WITH ME?

YOU WILL, OF COURSE, TELL HER IN NO UNCERTAIN TERMS THAT YOU ARE NOT INTERESTED, RIGHT?
HUH? WELL... YEAH... I GUESS... I MEAN, YEAH...
ROMEO, ROMEO, WHEREFORE ART THOU ROMEO?!
I'M *NOT* ROMEO, I'M ÔTANI!! NOW JUST LEAVE ME ALONE!
FWEE FWEE
...OH GOSH.
POOR MIMI. WONDER IF SHE'S OKAY...
SO HEYYY... WHAT'RE YOU GOING TO DO?
See you tomorrow!
GUESS I'LL STOP BY THERE AGAIN WHEN I GET HOME.

AND IF SHE COMES OUT TO SEE YOU THIS TIME, ARE YOU REALLY GOING TO TELL HER THERE'S NO WAY?
WHAT ELSE WOULD I SAY?
WELL... GOSH...
HEY, ISN'T THAT...
MIMI...?
ULP
HEY!!
MIMI!!

FWAP
MIMI-CHAN...
COME BACK HERE...!
WAIT, ŌTANI. LET *ME* GO TALK TO HER!
DASH
HUH?!
WAIT A SEC...
I KNOW...
...EXACTLY WHAT IT'S LIKE.

I'M SORRY.
I DIDN'T WANT TO SEE ÔTANI EITHER, AFTER I TOLD HIM HOW I FELT.
DASH
I TOTALLY AVOIDED HIM, BECAUSE I WAS SCARED TO DEATH HE'D REJECT ME.
UM...

GLARE
KES
YI
Uh... Umm...
...WHAT?
YOU WANNA FIGHT? YOU COME AFTER ME TO DUKE IT OUT?
NO...
NO, MIMI, THAT'S NOT IT AT ALL, I...
GWIP
DID ATCHAN SAY ANY-THING TO YOU?
HEH?
DID HE SAY ANYTHING ABOUT ME TO YOU?
IS HE MAD AT ME?

MAD AT YOU...? NO, OF COURSE HE ISN'T. HOW COME?
BECAUSE I CALLED HIM STUPID BY MISTAKE! I WASN'T THINKING AT ALL, AND IT JUST SLIPPED OUT!
YOU ARE SO STUPID.
ATCHAN!!
I CALL HIM STUPID ALL THE TIME, MIMI. WHAT'S THE BIG DEAL?
DON'T LUMP ME TOGETHER WITH YOUR DUMB SELF, BIMBO!!
AND ANYHOW, WHAT ELSE ARE WE SUPPOSED TO CALL HIM? HE IS STUPID.
I MEAN, MY GOD, THAT IDIOTIC EXPRESSION ON HIS FACE WHEN YOU TOLD HIM HOW YOU FEEL ABOUT HIM...
ATCHAN IS NOT STUPID, STUPID!!
ANYBODY'D BE SURPRISED IF SOMEONE SAID THAT TO THEM OUT OF THE BLUE!!
IT WAS MY FAULT FOR BLURTING IT OUT TO HIM LIKE THAT!!

DON'T EVER CALL ATCHAN STUPID IN FRONT OF ME AGAIN!!
NO, DON'T EVER CALL HIM STUPID AGAIN, PERIOD!! WHAT'S YOUR PROBLEM?!
HUH?
THIS GIRL REALLY LOVES ÔTANI A LOT.
...WOW.

YOU CALL HIM NAMES AND THEN CALL YOURSELF HIS GIRLFRIEND?! SCUM!!
OH, UH...
Well...
AND ANYHOW, LIKE YOU'RE A ROCKET SCIENTIST?! PATHETIC PINHEAD!!
YOU'RE THE DUMBEST PERSON I'VE EVER MET!! YOU'RE SO STUPID YOU MAKE COWS LOOK...
hanh
KOI...
...ZUMI
...
AND...
MI...
...MI...?

WAAAAAH!
WHAT'RE YOU DOING HERE, ATCHAN?! STUPID!!
DASH
OH NO! MIMI!! MIMI?!
WAS THAT...
...REALLY MIMI JUST NOW...?
...
OH GOSH. NOW WHAT...?

How ya doin'?

DID YOU STRAIGHTEN THINGS OUT WITH MIMI?

CHAPTER 32

NO. I GO OVER THERE, I CALL HER UP, SHE WON'T TALK TO ME.
I WAS AFRAID OF THAT...
YOU'RE SO STUPID YOU MAKE COWS LOOK...
CAT'S OUT OF THE BAG...
SHE MUST BE SO DEPRESSED...
...NOW THAT YOU'VE SEEN WHAT SHE'S REALLY LIKE.
hanh
WHADDAYA MEAN, "REALLY LIKE"?
YOU SAYING THE MIMI I KNOW IS A BIG FAKE?
THIS MIMI
WELL, I DON'T KNOW ABOUT "FAKE"...

IT'S MORE LIKE SHE WANTS TO BE CUTE AND SWEET IN FRONT OF THE GUY SHE LIKES, LIKE EVERY GIRL DOES.
...LIKE *EVERY* GIRL DOES? NOT VERY CONVINCING WHEN YOU SAY IT.

WHY NOT? I'M TOTALLY CUTE AND SWEET AROUND YOU, AREN'T I?

YOU'RE GROSSING ME OUT.

WHADDAYA MEAN, *GROSSING YOU OUT?!*

WHAT EXACTLY IS CUTE AND SWEET ABOUT YOU RIGHT NOW?

SEE? LIKE I SAID.

HEY! THAT'S BECAUSE *YOU ALWAYS SAY THE WRONG THING!!*

OH, WHO CARES ABOUT THAT?!
WHAT'RE YOU GOING TO DO ABOUT MIMI?!
NOT MUCH I *CAN* DO IF SHE WON'T SEE ME OR TALK TO ME.
OH...
I GUESS NOT...

...SO THEN WHAT...?

hmmm

...

WHY'RE YOU SO WORRIED ABOUT HER, ANYWAY? YOU HARDLY EVEN *KNOW* MIMI.

WHAT'RE YOU GETTING SO INVOLVED FOR?

LOOK, JUST GIVE HER TIME TO CHILL A LITTLE, AND SHE'LL PROBABLY COME OUT BY HERSELF, WITHOUT ME BANGING ON THE DOOR.

...

...YEAH ...

...GUESS HE'S RIGHT ABOUT THAT.

BUT STILL...
IT'S JUST THAT I CAN TOTALLY RELATE TO HER...
TO WHO?
WITH THAT GIRL MIMI.
I KNOW EXACTLY WHAT SHE'S GOING THROUGH.
PLUS, WHEN I THINK HOW MUCH *WORSE* SHE'LL FEEL AFTER HE GIVES HER THE "SORRY, BUT" SPIEL, IT JUST KILLS ME.
Well, that's just too bad.
LOOK, *YOU'D* FEEL A LOT WORSE THAN THAT IF HE *DIDN'T* GIVE HER THE "SORRY, BUT" SPIEL, RISA.
JUST STOP WORRYING ABOUT HER. LET ÔTANI TAKE CARE OF IT.
THAT'S ACTUALLY THE BIGGEST WORRY OF ALL.
HE'S THE MOST CLUELESS GUY IN ALL OF JAPAN WHEN IT COMES TO GIRLS' FEELINGS.

I MEAN, MY GOD! HE'S DENSE, HE'S OBLIVIOUS... I DON'T KNOW HOW MANY TIMES HE RAKED ME OVER THE COALS WITH HIS STUPIDITY.
OOPS, WERE YOU BEHIND ME JUST NOW?
YOU'RE SO TINY I DIDN'T NOTICE, SORRY.
HEY! WHAT KIND OF BOZO DO YOU THINK I AM, ANYWAY?!
WANT ME TO RAKE YOU OVER THE COALS RIGHT NOW?!
bzzzzzz
POOR MIMI...
HOPE *SHE* ISN'T SPREAD OUT OVER THE COALS AT THIS VERY MOMENT...
ZHWOO
HEY.

GLOOOOOOM
...Umm... Mimi...?
GLARE
YIPES
TURN
Mimi-chan... Umm... Are you okay?
MEANING WHAT?
Well, you know... I thought you might be kinda bumming after what happened...
YOU WANT ME TO BE BUMMED OUT, DON'T YOU, DOGFACE? WELL, I'M NOT.
I'M SPITTIN' MAD. BECAUSE THIS IS ALL YOUR STUPID FAULT, PEABRAIN.
HEH?!

MY WHOLE LIFE I'VE BEEN SWEET IN FRONT OF HIM, AND THEN YOU COME ALONG AND I'M BUSTED!! ALL THAT HARD WORK DOWN THE DRAIN!!
Uh...
YOU PLANNED THAT, DIDN'T YOU?! YOU MADE ME LOSE IT ON PURPOSE AND THEN CALLED HIM SO HE'D SEE IT, DIDN'T YOU?!
No, of course not...
DON'T LIE TO ME, SCUM!! YOU'RE GONNA PAY FOR THIS!!
Urgh!
HEY!!
IT'S ÔTANI!!
WHAT?!
FOOLED YOU...
...DON'T YOU MESS WITH ME, YOU STUPID COW.
WANT ME TO COME SHAVE OFF YOUR EYE-BROWS WHILE YOU'RE ASLEEP?! HUH?!
UH, MAYBE THIS ISN'T A GOOD PLACE FOR THIS.
WHY DON'T WE GET SOME-THING TO DRINK SOME-WHERE? ON ME!
YEAH, RIGHT. ON YOU, MIZ FIFTY YEN.
I HAVE MONEY TODAY!! I DO!!
THERE!
NOW BIG SISTER RISA CAN CHEER POOR LITTLE MIMI UP A BIT.

I'LL HAVE A ONE-POUND SLAB OF YOUR BEST SIRLOIN STEAK.
MEDIUM-RARE. WITH A SALAD, RICE AND BLACK TEA.
IGNORE THAT, PLEASE! WE'LL HAVE TWO FREE-REFILL SOFT DRINKS.
Tch!
CHEAP-SKATE. TIGHT-WAD.
SHUDDUP, DOG-BREATH.
...
hee hee
SO HEY, MIMI, WHAT WERE YOU DOING WHEN I BUMPED INTO YOU?
HM?
...HEY, IS THAT...
...THE DAILY CARTON OF MILK YOU BUY FOR ŌTANI?

FWAP

RUSTLE

NONE OF YOUR STUPID BEESWAX.

...

TEE HEE!

WHAT'S SO DARN FUNNY, YOU DUMB DITZ?! YOU LAUGHING AT ME?!

NO... NOT AT ALL.

I JUST THOUGHT IT WAS SO CUTE.

YOU ***ARE*** LAUGHING AT ME, YOU PIG!!

LOOK, IT ALL STARTED GOING SCREWY WHEN ***YOU*** SHOWED UP!! THIS IS ALL ***YOUR*** FAULT!!

IF ***YOU*** WEREN'T AROUND, I COULD'VE KEPT UP THE SWEETIE-PIE ACT FOR AS LONG AS I WANTED!!

IF ***YOU*** WEREN'T AROUND, I'D NEVER HAVE...

BLURTING IT OUT LIKE THAT...
THAT WAS SO STUPID AND HUMILIATING...
...I'D NEVER HAVE TOLD ATCHAN I LOVE HIM IN THAT DORKY WAY...
...WHAT?
...MIMI-CHAN...
I LOVE YOU A THOUSAND TIMES MORE THAN SHE DOES, ATCHAN!!
...
WHAT CAN I DO TO MAKE HER FEEL BETTER...?
GRR
WHAT'RE YOU GONNA DO ABOUT IT?! MAKE IT UP TO ME!!
MAKE IT UP... TO YOU?

LOOK, THANKS TO YOU EVERY-THING'S GONE WRONG FOR ME!!

HEH?

SO THE LEAST YOU CAN DO IS MAKE UP FOR IT, RIGHT?!

...

YEAH. BY LETTING ME HAVE ATCHAN!!

BUT... I CAN'T...

WELL, JEEZ! IT'S *MY WHOLE LIFE,* OKAY?! DON'T YOU FEEL SORRY FOR ME?!

I DON'T KNOW WHAT TO DO ANYMORE! I CAN'T EVEN FACE HIM ANYMORE!!

...MIMI...

I'M SORRY.

BUT...

EVEN SO...

...I REALLY DON'T WANT MIMI TO FEEL HOW I FELT AFTER ÔTANI TURNED ME DOWN.

LET HER HAVE HIM...?

LET HER HAVE ÔTANI ...?

I JUST CAN'T DO THAT.

...LISTEN, MIMI.

WELL, WHY NOT?!

WHY NOT...?

BECAUSE I REALLY LOVE ÔTANI TOO.

WELL, *I* LOVE HIM *MORE* THAN YOU DO!!

NO... *I* LOVE HIM JUST AS MUCH!!

NO, *I* LOVE HIM ***MORE!!***

NO, *I* LOVE HIM MORE!!

LOOK, IF YOU LOVE HIM SO MUCH, TELL HIM THAT AGAIN!! NOT BLURTING IT OUT, BUT PROPERLY!!

I MEAN, YOU SAID YOU WERE GOING TO TAKE HIM AWAY FROM ME! WHY SHOULD I JUST ***GIVE*** HIM TO YOU?!

...

...

I'LL DO THAT. THANKS FOR THE TIP.

K-TUNK

DON'T BLAME ME IF YOU REGRET IT.

ULP

THIS TIME, I'M GONNA DO IT RIGHT.

AND HE'S GONNA FORGET YOU EVER EXISTED.

KLAK

WAIT! MIMI-CHAN!!

K-TUNK

I CAN'T CANCEL THAT ORDER... SO WILL YOU STAY AND HAVE YOUR DRINK?
...
...DARN IT.
I GOT HER ALL PUMPED UP ABOUT STEALING HIM FROM ME AGAIN.
SHLRRRRP
WELL, FINE.
IF SHE'S GOING AFTER HIM FOR REAL, THEN I SURE DON'T PLAN TO HAND HIM OVER JUST LIKE THAT.
SHE'S GONNA HAVE TO FIGHT ME, TOOTH AND NAIL!!
HUNH?!

SO *THAT'S* WHY SHE SHOWED UP THIS MORNING WITH TEN CARTONS OF MILK!!

WHAT DID YOU HAVE TO STIR THINGS UP LIKE THAT FOR?!

WELL, GOSH! SHE ACTUALLY ***DEMANDED*** THAT I LET HER HAVE YOU!!

OF ALL THE DUMB THINGS...

WELL, THE REASON STUFF LIKE THIS HAPPENS IS *YOU* DIDN'T SET HER STRAIGHT RIGHT AWAY!

BELIEVE ME, I'M TRYING! BUT FIRST SHE WON'T SEE ME OR TALK TO ME, AND THEN WHEN SHE FINALLY DOES, SHE'S HANDING ME TEN CARTONS OF MILK! IT'S NOT EXACTLY EASY!

DID SHE SAY ANY-THING TO YOU THIS MORNING?

OH YEAH. SHE DID.

SHE WANTS TO GO OUT THIS SATURDAY.

WITH YOU AND ME BOTH.

...HUH?

...THE THREE OF US?

I SAID NO WAY, BUT SHE WOULDN'T LISTEN. SAID SHE'D TALK TO YOU ABOUT IT HERSELF IF I DON'T.

RISA! THAT'S A GAUNTLET IF THERE EVER WAS ONE!

SHE THROWS IT DOWN, YOU GOTTA TAKE IT UP!

A GAUNTLET...

OH...SO THAT'S WHAT IT IS...

HEY, GUYS. HOLD ON A SECOND HERE.

ALL RIGHT, ŌTANI! YOU TELL HER I'M TAKING UP HER GAUNTLET, AND NO MISTAKE!

COME ON, YOU GUYS, GET A GRIP...

THAT'S RIGHT, RISA! YOU GO, GIRL!!

ŌTANI'S LOVE IS MINE AND MINE ALONE!!

H-HEY...

GO, RISA!! VICTORY SHALL BE YOURS!!
GO, RISA!! WE'RE ON YOUR SIDE!!
JUST WATCH ME, MY FRIENDS!!
WILL YOU GUYS JUST HOLD ON?!
WELL, I LOVE HIM MORE THAN YOU DO!!
...I DON'T THINK SO, MIMI.
NOT TO MENTION...
...I CLAWED MY WAY UP HERE AFTER GETTING REJECTED BY HIM ONCE.
THERE IS NO WAY I'M LOSING TO YOU!!
tweet
chirp
chirp

...
I SAID, GET OFF OF ME!! LEAVE ME ALONE!
OH, COME ON, WHAT'S WRONG WITH IT?
HERE SHE IS. THE ENEMY!
LOOK, MIMI, WILL YOU JUST...
OKAY, ATCHAN, NOW BE QUIET FOR A SEC!
I'LL SHOW YOU WHICH OF US REALLY LOVES ATCHAN MOST, SO THERE. JUST WATCH ME.
GRR

Well, I guess this is where I say good-bye.

This volume's bonus pages were originally a supplement that came with that month's issue of Bessatsu Margaret. All kinds of people helped to make it a really great supplement, so we've reproduced its pages virtually as-is for you here. Heh heh!

Oh, and thank you everybody for all of your letters. Emails that get sent to the Bessatsu Margaret homepage get printed out like this

and sent to me by post, so I get to read all of them. A lot of people ask for a postal address in their emails, so here it is:

Aya Nakahara
c/o Shojo Beat
295 Bay St.
San Francisco, CA 94133

Thank you
And see you again!!

Aya 2004. 6

PFFFT
MUST'VE BEEN A GREAT DATE IF HE DOESN'T WANT TO HEAR ABOUT IT!
I... AM NOT LOSING TO THIS OBNOX-IOUS MIDDLE-SCHOOLER!
GWIP
RISA LOVES ATCHAN MORE THAN MIMI DOES, SO THERE!!
KLUTCH
WILL YOU TWO JUST CUT IT OUT?! LAY OFF OF ME!!
PAKOON
BWEENG

BEEP
BIP
BIP
BIP
BIP
OH, WOW. HMM.
I'VE NEVER BEEN TO ONE OF THESE PLACES BEFORE.
GLANCE
BUT I'M NOT INTO GAMING, SO THIS ISN'T GONNA BE ANY FUN...

WHERE DO YOU WANNA START? WHAT DO YOU WANNA DO?
THUD
THUD
HEY, THAT ONE THERE'S FREE! AIR HOCKEY, YEAH!! LET'S GO!
THUD
THUD
UM, ATCHAN ...?!
THUD
WAHOOO
SHWAKK
KRAKK
WAHAHOO
YABADOO? YABADOO-BIDOO!
WAHOOO!! WAHAHOO-LAHEY!
WAHOOO
WAHOOO
UH-OH
GLANCE
ÔTANI? WHAT HAPPENED TO MIMI?
ULP
HUH?
OH.

COME PLAY WITH US, MIMI! IT'S TOTALLY FUN!
...
THUNK
...?
blah

HEY KOIZUMI, YOU LOST SO YOU HAVE TO PAY A PENALTY!
TREAT US, PLEASE!
Darn it!
TO WHAT?
A COLA!
OKAY. AND FOR YOU, MIMI?
...
...MELON SODA.
COMING RIGHT UP!
DON'T TRIP AND FALL WHEN YOU BRING IT, CLUMSY!
LEAVE ME ALONE!
...TRIP AND FALL?
LAST TIME WE WERE HERE, SHE TRIPPED HOLDING A TRAY WITH OUR EMPTIES AND GOT ICE CUBES AND STUFF ALL OVER THE FLOOR.

WHAT A DORK, RIGHT?
WHAT?
...WHAT'S SO FUNNY ABOUT TRIPPING AND MAKING A BIG MESS? IT'S PATHETIC.
THAT GOOFY SMILE ON YOUR FACE JUST NOW, ATCHAN. I'VE NEVER SEEN YOU LOOK LIKE THAT BEFORE.
...ER.
I LOOKED GOOFY?
koff
YEAH. YOU LOOKED REALLY DUMB.

EXCUSE ME?
THE ATCHAN I KNOW IS COOL, NOT GOOFY.
YEAH, SO? I'M COOL RIGHT NOW. I'M ALWAYS COOL.
NOT TODAY! GOING "WAHAHOO" AND GETTING SO INTO THOSE GAMES LIKE SOME KIND OF IDIOT.
Whatever!
...
WHO'S SUCH A BIG IDIOT?
...THAT'S 'CUZ KOIZUMI'S SUCH A BIG IDIOT. IT KINDA RUBS OFF ON ME.

HEY, WHATCHA GOT THERE, KOIZUMI? BESIDES THE SODAS.
ICE CREAM.
OOH! LEMME HAVE SOME, LEMME HAVE SOME!
I FIGURED YOU'D WANT TO TRY, SO I GOT THREE SPOONS.
I THINK IT'S A NEW FLAVOR.
PWOP
OMIGOD!!
THIS IS AMAAAZ-ING!! WHAT *IS* IT?!
WHEEE
YOGURT SOME-THING...
OMIGOD, IT'S *SO* YUM!!
SQUEAL
SQUEAL
THUMP

TRY THIS, MIMI!!
NO THANKS!!
I'M GOING HOME!!
WHAT?!
HUH?! YOU'RE THE ONE WHO WANTED TO GO OUT TOGETHER IN THE FIRST PLACE!
WHAT'S GOING ON?
IS SOME-THING THE MATTER...?

WAIT A MINUTE, MIMI!!
...IF I DON'T TELL YOU THIS NOW, YOU'LL GIVE ME THE RUNAROUND AGAIN AND I'LL NEVER BE ABLE TO TELL YOU.
!
ÔTANI... IS HE GOING TO...

DON'T TELL ME!!
YOU'RE GOING TO TOTALLY REJECT ME, AREN'T YOU?!
OH, MIMI...
MIMI!
LISTEN TO ME.
NOOO! STOP!!
NO! I AM NOT LISTEN-ING!!

I...
NOOOOO!!
...OF YOU AS...
GYAAAAGH!!
...SO ...
I-DON'T-HEAR-YOU-!!
MIMI!!
WAAAAAAAAGH!!
...
KA-POW
YOU MEAT-HEAD!!

WHA... HEY...
WHADJA DO *THAT* FOR?!
WHAT HAPPENED TO ALL THAT FIGHT YOU HAD IN YOU?!
WEREN'T YOU TELLING ME YOU LOVE ÔTANI MORE THAN I DO?! HUH?!
YOU'RE JUST ALL TALK AND NO WALK! IN FACT, ALL YOU DO IS TALK AND *RUN!!*
HOW WOULD YOU KNOW WHAT IT'S LIKE? YOU'RE HIS GIRLFRIEND! YOU DON'T KNOW HOW MUCH IT HURTS TO HEAR...
I *DO* KNOW!! BECAUSE WAY BEFORE I WAS HIS GIRLFRIEND, I TOLD HIM I LOVED HIM AND HE JILTED ME!!
...WHAT?
HE SAID SORRY, BUT HE COULDN'T GO OUT WITH ME OR THINK OF ME THAT WAY. BUT I COULDN'T GET OVER HIM, SO I KEPT TRYING!

...NO WAY.
YES WAY. AND NOW THAT WE'RE FINALLY GOING OUT? ALL HE DOES IS CALL ME STUPID AND GROSS AND STUFF LIKE THAT! NOT TO MENTION, WHEN I ASKED HIM WHY HE'S GOING OUT WITH ME, HE SAID IT "JUST HAPPENED," OKAY?!
I MEAN, THE WAY HE TREATS ME, I DON'T EVEN KNOW IF HE LOVES ME IN THE FIRST PLACE!
UH...!
WHAT THE HECK'RE YOU...
BUT YOU KNOW WHAT? I DON'T CARE! BECAUSE I'M TOTALLY NUTS ABOUT HIM, AND JUST BEING WITH HIM IS ENOUGH FOR ME!!

I'M NOT HANDING ÔTANI OVER TO ANYBODY. ESPECIALLY NOT TO A TOTAL WUSS...
...WHO RUNS AWAY FROM HIM BECAUSE SHE CAN'T FACE REJECTION!
HMPH
TROMP
TROMP
TROMP

...HEY, ATCHAN...
PFFFF
WHAT'S WITH THAT GIRLFRIEND OF YOURS?!
SHE'S KINDA CRAZY, I SWEAR!! I REALLY MEAN THAT!!
hee hee hee
...
SHE'S PRETTY FUNNY, ISN'T SHE?
WHAT'RE YOU LAUGHING ABOUT?!
SHE PUNCHED ME IN THE FACE, OKAY?!
YEAH, WELL, SHE'S PUNCHED ME IN THE FACE TONS OF TIMES.

NO WAAAY!!
I KNOW HOW HARD IT IS TO HAVE THE GUY YOU LIKE TURN YOU DOWN.
BUT...
...I ALSO KNOW THAT IF YOU KEEP TRYING, YOU CAN CHANGE HOW HE FEELS ABOUT YOU.
SHE'S REALLY...
...KINDA DIFFERENT, ISN'T SHE...
YEAH, SHE'S PRETTY DIFFERENT, ALL RIGHT.
NEVER A DULL MOMENT AROUND HER, THAT'S FOR SURE.
...HEY, ATCHAN?
DO YOU LOVE HER?

I'M NUTS ABOUT HER.
...WELL, THEN OBVIOUSLY I DON'T STAND A CHANCE WITH YOU. 'CUZ THERE'S NO WAY I COULD EVER BE THAT STUPID!
MAYBE NOT!

WHY DON'T YOU EVER TELL HER YOU LOVE HER, THOUGH? YOU SHOULD.
NO WAY!!
ARE YOU KIDDING ME?! NOT MY STYLE!!
FTAP
MIMI! MIMI-CHAN!!
FTAP
FTAP
I'M SORRY!!
I AM SO SORRY ABOUT SOCKING YOU LIKE THAT! ARE YOU OKAY?!
HANH
HANH
HANH
HANH

HA-HA! HAHAHAHA!
HUH?
I DON'T KNOW HOW MUCH ÔTANI LOVES ME, OR WHAT HE SEES IN ME IN THE FIRST PLACE...
...BUT THERE'S ONE THING I KNOW FOR SURE. NOBODY IN THE WORLD...
...LOVES HIM AS MUCH AS I DO. SO THERE!
《...to be continued》

SPECIAL ISSUE

●Cover art: Aya Nakahara

Special price: ¥0

CHOCK-FULL OF FUN & EXCITING FEATURES!!

The Mighty Girls: What do they do? We'll tell you! Also... Wanted: New members!

Remedial Love★Com 101! Compre-hension guaranteed or your money back!!

HOW SERIOUS A FAN ARE YOU? FIND OUT WITH...

THE LOVE★COM DETAILS TEST

DON'T MISS THE AWESOME BONUS SERIES:

OSAKA FIGHTERS

THE LOVE★COM RANGERS!

LOVE IT OR HATE IT, IT'S A...
SPECIAL EPISODE
OSAKA FIGHTERS
THE LOVE★COM RANGERS!
L★C
L★C
L★C
L★C
The Love Com All-Stars in Another Guise?!
Episode 21
"Kong Joins the Dark Side?! The Hidden Code in the Mid-Term Exams"
By Supreme Commander of the Osaka Fighter Brigade
Aya Nakahara
KLIK
DA-DOOT
KLIK
KLIK
KLIK
KLIK
KLIK

KLATTER
CAPTAIN!
IT'S A MONSTER ALERT! A MONSTER HAS BEEN DETECTED IN THE FACULTY ROOM!!
DA-DOOT
DA-DOOT
TAKKA
TAKKA
DA-DOOT
TAKKA
WHAT?!
GET THE WORD OUT TO EVERYBODY, NOBU-CHAN. RIGHT AWAY!!
KLATTER
CAPTAIN
KA-CHAK
ROGER!
IT'S ME. ARE YOU ALL THERE?!
A MONSTER'S BEEN DETECTED IN THE FACULTY ROOM!
TRANSFORM YOURSELVES INTO RANGERS AND GO STRAIGHT THERE!

ROGER!
Ohhh! Where are you going?
TRANS...
...FORM!!
PWOOOO
OOOF
THE LOVE★COM RANGERS!!

FACULTY ROOM
WHAM
WHERE'S THE MONSTER ?!
SENPAI, LOOK! OVER THERE!!
OMIGOD!
PHLAP
MWAHA-HAHAHA-HAHA! I'M MAKING THIS THE HARDEST TEST YOU GUYS EVER SAW!
YOU WON'T MAKE HEADS OR TAILS OF IT UNLESS YOU REALLY STUDY!
KONG!!

HOLY MOLY!! LOOK AT THIS!!
KRICH KRICH KRICH KRICH
nyar-har-har-har
THESE QUESTIONS ARE TOTALLY HARD!!
I can't even tell what they're about!!
THE USABA-RASHI LEAGUE HAS GOT TO BE BEHIND THIS!!
OF ALL THE LOW THINGS...!! HOW DARE HE DO THIS TO US?!
KONG'S FALLEN INTO THEIR CLUTCHES!!
You saw the symbol on his forehead?!
WELL, WE'RE NOT LETTING HIM GET AWAY WITH THIS!!
HUH?!
NOT SO FAST, MY FRIENDS.
MIGHTY... THE SUPREME COMMANDER OF THE USABARASHI LEAGUE!!
MMH MMH MMH MMH MMH.

FWAK
YOU THREE THERE ARE ALL SENIORS, AND YET ALL YOU DO IS GOOF OFF AND HAVE FUN EVERY DAY, DO YOU NOT?
FWIK
JOK
FWIK
ARGH ...!
I DON'T THINK I'VE EVER SEEN ANY OF YOU STUDYING THIS YEAR. DO YOU THINK YOU'LL BE ABLE TO GRADUATE AT THIS RATE?
WORGH!!
AND NONE OF YOU EVEN HOLDS DOWN A PART-TIME JOB, YET YOU ALL SEEM TO HAVE QUITE EXTENSIVE WARDROBES.
GYAAAAAAGH!!
NIK
SENPAIS!!
WHAT'S THE MATTER WITH YOU? YOU HAVE TO FIGHT BACK!!
SHOOOOO
That's right, Mighty, those subjects are taboo and you know it...
OWWW, THAT HURT.
HANH
HANH
THAT WAS BELOW THE BELT, MIGHTY!!
MMH MMH MMH MMH MMH.

NOW, MISTER KONG!!
KONG KONG KONG KONG KONG KONG KONG KONG
FINISH THEM OFF!!
NONE OF YOU IS GETTING INTO COLLEGE, THAT'S FOR SURE!
PHLAP PHLAP
I'LL SEE TO IT YOU'LL HAVE YOUR HANDS FULL JUST TRYING TO GRADU-ATE!
SENPAIS! DON'T TELL ME YOU'RE GIVING UP JUST LIKE THAT?!
COME ON! WE'RE THE LOVE☆COM RANGERS! WE FIGHT FOR LOVE AND JUSTICE!!
L★C

FIN ★ A punch line reminiscent of Risa's notorious "Not my Summon Monsters too!"?!

Comprehension guaranteed, or your money back!

REMEDIAL LOVE★COM 101 THE REAL BASICS

Today's class is about a story that takes place in Osaka and features a tall-and-short comedy team.

YOU'LL BE TESTED ON THIS AT THE END. DON'T SAY I DIDN'T WARN YOU.

The Basics #1

Get all the facts on Risa and Ôtani!

Risa Koizumi and Atsushi Ôtani are the main characters of this story!! ... But that much you *do* know, don't you?

Which of them is a better student?

	Ôtani	Risa
1st year:	Failed both mid-terms and finals	Got D minus on both mid-terms and finals
2nd year:	Both avoid having to attend remedial summer school	
3rd year:	Both ordered by Kong to attend remedial summer school.	
	Test score: 6/50	Test score: 4/50

CONCLUSION: THEY'RE BOTH TERRIBLE STUDENTS

What are their families like?

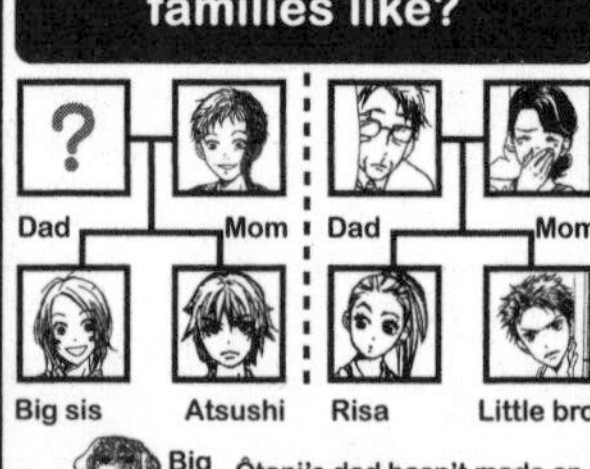

Big dog

Ôtani's dad hasn't made an appearance in the story yet. Does that bother you?

Why're they called All Hanshin-Kyojin in the first place?

① The big difference in their heights

Ôtani
1st year 5'1"
2nd year 5'1.25"
Name means "big valley," but he's very little. Also very dense when it comes to romance.

Risa
Little bro
1st year 5'7"
2nd year 5'8"
A jumbo-gal. Basically a funny girl, with almost zero sex appeal?!

② Their constant squabbling

The perfect timing with which they trade insults is professional comedian-class. Both reasons are shared by the Yoshimoto manzai team All Hanshin-Kyojin.

HOW ABOUT KOIZUMI AND ÔTANI, WHO GET ALONG SO WELL THEY CAN CONVERSE USING ONLY EYE CONTACT?

WHY US?!

③ Because Kong, their teacher, gave them the moniker.

④ And the whole class wholeheartedly agreed.

YOU WON BY A LANDSLIDE!
SO THAT'S DECIDED! CONGRATULATIONS!

VOTED CLASS REPRESENTATIVES FOR THREE YEARS IN A ROW!

This is why they're called "All Hanshin-Kyojin!"

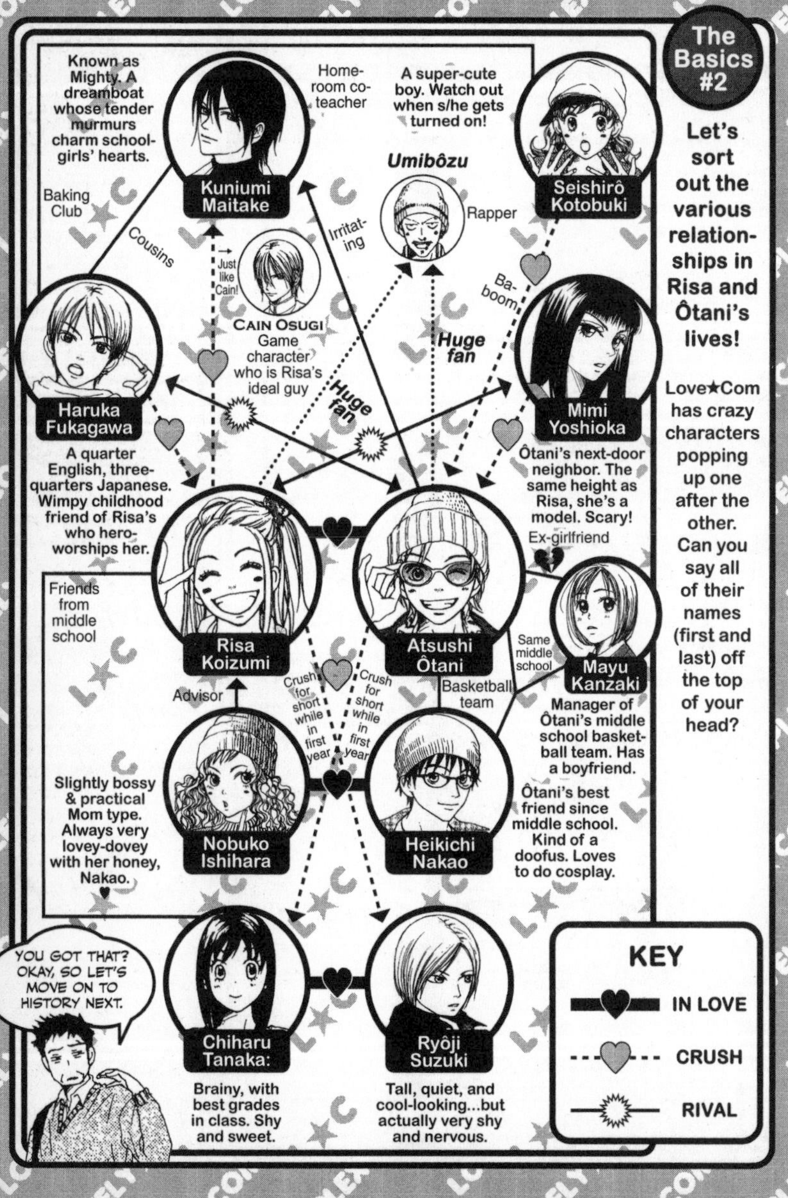
The Basics #2
Let's sort out the various relationships in Risa and Ôtani's lives!
Love★Com has crazy characters popping up one after the other. Can you say all of their names (first and last) off the top of your head?
Known as Mighty. A dreamboat whose tender murmurs charm schoolgirls' hearts.
Home-room co-teacher
Kuniumi Maitake
A super-cute boy. Watch out when s/he gets turned on!
Seishirô Kotobuki
Umibôzu
Rapper
Baking Club
Cousins
Just like Cain!
Irritating
CAIN OSUGI Game character who is Risa's ideal guy
Ba-boom
Huge fan
Huge fan
Haruka Fukagawa
A quarter English, three-quarters Japanese. Wimpy childhood friend of Risa's who hero-worships her.
Mimi Yoshioka
Ôtani's next-door neighbor. The same height as Risa, she's a model. Scary!
Ex-girlfriend
Friends from middle school
Risa Koizumi
Atsushi Ôtani
Same middle school
Mayu Kanzaki
Manager of Ôtani's middle school basketball team. Has a boyfriend.
Advisor
Crush for short while in first year
Crush for short while in first year
Basketball team
Slightly bossy & practical Mom type. Always very lovey-dovey with her honey, Nakao.
Nobuko Ishihara
Heikichi Nakao
Ôtani's best friend since middle school. Kind of a doofus. Loves to do cosplay.
YOU GOT THAT? OKAY, SO LET'S MOVE ON TO HISTORY NEXT.
Chiharu Tanaka:
Brainy, with best grades in class. Shy and sweet.
Ryôji Suzuki
Tall, quiet, and cool-looking...but actually very shy and nervous.
KEY
IN LOVE
CRUSH
RIVAL
LOVELY★COMPLEX

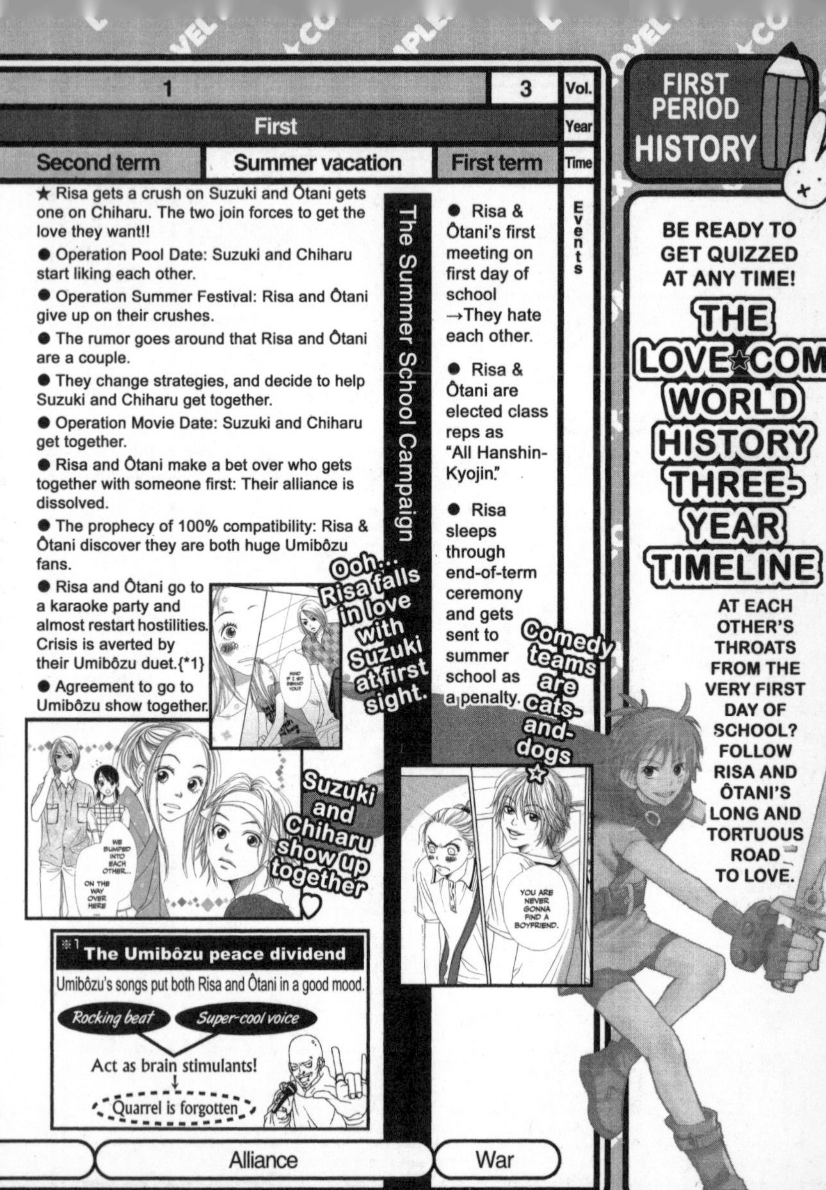

FIRST PERIOD HISTORY

BE READY TO GET QUIZZED AT ANY TIME!

THE LOVE★COM WORLD HISTORY THREE-YEAR TIMELINE

AT EACH OTHER'S THROATS FROM THE VERY FIRST DAY OF SCHOOL? FOLLOW RISA AND ÔTANI'S LONG AND TORTUOUS ROAD TO LOVE.

Vol.	3	1	
Year	First		
Time	First term	Summer vacation	Second term
Events	● Risa & Ôtani's first meeting on first day of school →They hate each other. ● Risa & Ôtani are elected class reps as "All Hanshin-Kyojin." ● Risa sleeps through end-of-term ceremony and gets sent to summer school as a penalty.	The Summer School Campaign	★ Risa gets a crush on Suzuki and Ôtani gets one on Chiharu. The two join forces to get the love they want!! ● Operation Pool Date: Suzuki and Chiharu start liking each other. ● Operation Summer Festival: Risa and Ôtani give up on their crushes. ● The rumor goes around that Risa and Ôtani are a couple. ● They change strategies, and decide to help Suzuki and Chiharu get together. ● Operation Movie Date: Suzuki and Chiharu get together. ● Risa and Ôtani make a bet over who gets together with someone first: Their alliance is dissolved. ● The prophecy of 100% compatibility: Risa & Ôtani discover they are both huge Umibôzu fans. ● Risa and Ôtani go to a karaoke party and almost restart hostilities. Crisis is averted by their Umibôzu duet.{*1} ● Agreement to go to Umibôzu show together.
	War	Alliance	

Comedy teams are cats-and-dogs☆
YOU ARE NEVER GONNA FIND A BOYFRIEND.
Ooh... Risa falls in love with Suzuki at first sight.
Suzuki and Chiharu show up together♡
WE BUMPED INTO EACH OTHER...
ON THE WAY OVER HERE

※1 **The Umibôzu peace dividend**

Umibôzu's songs put both Risa and Ôtani in a good mood.

Rocking beat / Super-cool voice

Act as brain stimulants!

↓

Quarrel is forgotten

2
First
Second term
Winter vacation
Third term
Spring vacation
First term
3
Second
The Ôtani Ex-Girlfriend Incident
★ Risa is shocked to find out that Ôtani had a girlfriend before!
● Ex-girlfriend sends message to Ôtani: Ôtani's heart is recaptured?
● The Umibôzu Christmas concert: Risa's heart is captured by Ôtani?!
● New Year's shrine visit: Risa thinks Ôtani's ex wants to get back together with him. This later turns out to be a big misunderstanding.
His ex looks just like Chiharu!
GOSH...
THAT WAS FREAKY...
Ôtani chooses Risa over his ex and...?
LOOK.
WE PLANNED TO DO THIS BEFORE SHE EVER SHOWED UP, RIGHT?
The Haruka Invasion
★ Risa's childhood friend Haruka arrives and moves in on Risa!!
● Haruka declares war on Ôtani.
● Ôtani refuses Risa's "just friends" Valentine
● Haruka asks Risa to be his girlfriend: She refuses.
● Attack of the yakuza dog: Haruka begs Ôtani for help, takes back declaration of war. Risa starts to fall for Ôtani?!
Ôtani as "captured space alien"
THE CAPTURED SPACE ALIEN.
Haruka's crazy about Risa!
YOU'VE BEEN MY HERO SINCE WAY BACK, RISA.
I WANT YOU TO BE COOL. ALL THE TIME.
YOUR HERO?
The Seiko Attack
★ Risa & Ôtani are in same class for second year in a row. Alluring new student Seiko falls for Ôtani, and hard!
● Seiko gives Ôtani a very public kiss: Risa is deeply perturbed.
● Seiko turns out to be a boy: Ôtani dies of shock.
● Seiko decides to keep trying: Tells Risa they're rivals.
● Risa becomes sure she's in love with Ôtani!!
Seiko's pheromones go bonkers!
I'VE JUST FALLEN IN LOVE! ♡
FROM HEAVEN...
TA
DAH
OUR TIME HAS COME!!
▼
...to Hell
Conflict
The Age of the Little Man

Vol.
4
5
Year
Second
Time
Summer vacation
Second term
Winter vacation
Third term
Spring vacation
Events
The Long Confession of Love Campaign
★ Risa initiates her attack!!
● The Cafeteria Conference: Nobu becomes Risa's prime minister (*2) and enlists the support of Nakao, Suzuki and Chiharu.
● The Battle of the Beach: Washout
● The Fireworks Showdown (Risa's birthday): Dud.(*3)
● Risa Spooks Ôtani at School Festival: Message gets through.
● Class trip to Hokkaido / Bear Curry Incident: Risa takes heavy losses.
● Umibôzu family surfaces in Hakodate: Risa is inspired!
The Flaunting of Inner Boobies Period
★ Using sexiness (?) as her weapon, Risa tries to turn the tide!
● Confinement in storage closet incident: Although this is how Ôtani and Mayu got together, nothing happens when it's Risa.
● New Year's Eve karaoke night: Risa and Ôtani have a great time, but then Mayu breaks up with her boyfriend!
● Junior high basketball reunion crisis: Guys try to get Ôtani and Mayu back together, but fail.
● Re-emergence of Haruka: Exposes Ôtani's rejection of Risa to the whole class.
● The Valentine's Day confrontation: Ôtani refuses Risa's "for real" Valentine, but she forces it on him anyway.
● The visit to Ôtani's home on his birthday → Risa meets Ôtani's mom → Risa moves in on Ôtani → Ôtani gives Risa her first kiss ever!
● The Umibôzu show tragedy: Ôtani doesn't remember the kiss. Risa is outraged.
Risa finally tells Ôtani how she feels, but...?
DOESN'T IT EVER OCCUR TO YOU...
...EVEN FOR ONE SECOND...
...THAT IT MIGHT BE YOU?
The tears she'd been holding back spill over...
ÔTANI'S UM... UH, BEAR MEAT CURRY...
Gazing up at the night sky, Risa vows to keep fighting!
SORRY, BUT...
...I TAKE BACK WHAT I SAID ABOUT FORGETTING ANY OF THAT STUFF EVER HAPPENED.
AND I DON'T WANT YOU TO FORGET IT, EITHER.
Haruka vents his spleen at Ôtani's treatment of Risa!
WHAT?!
Did he kiss her because he was feverish?
※2 The Machinations of Prime Minister Nobu
Controlling Risa from the shadows, Nobu engineers her confession of love with such speed and skill that Ôtani remains completely unaware of her diplomacy...
Silencing inappropriate utterances!
Sending out control
Risa's Era of Great Striving

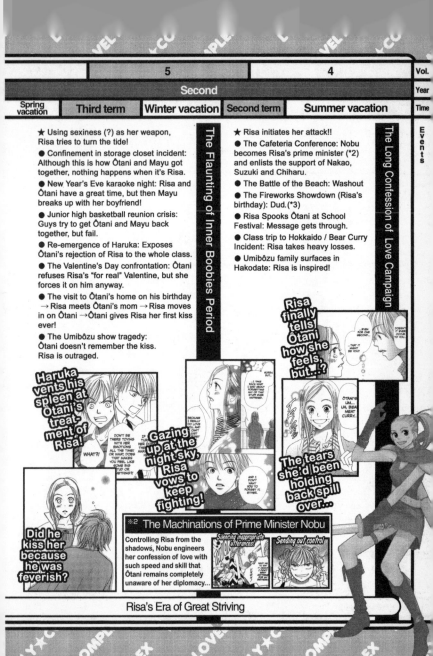

8	7	6

Third

First term

The Ôtani vs. Mighty Wars

★ Risa & Ôtani in same class for third year running. New homeroom co-teacher Mighty sets Risa's heart racing!

● The kiss that wasn't a kiss: Risa finds out Ôtani was trying to pick a rice grain out of her hair. She kisses him, sees no reaction, and vows she will quit loving him.

● Risa starts the Mighty Girls → Nobu blames Ôtani → Ôtani is furious.

● Ôtani declares Risa means nothing to him: Risa loses fighting spirit.

● Mighty casts a magical spell: Ôtani suddenly jealous?!

● Ôtani injured in basketball contest with Mighty: Names Risa his chauffeur.

● Ôtani tells Risa not to quit loving him: The Mighty Girls are disbanded.

The power of Mighty Magic?

Mighty is exactly like Cain! ♥

Summer vacation

The Ôtani Emotional Overthrow

★ Ôtani comes close to slaying Risa by telling her he needs her to be around him all the time, but she is asleep and doesn't hear. The attempt is a failure.

● Fireworks Festival (Risa's birthday): Ôtani kisses her.

● The Incident of the Introduction: Risa introduces Ôtani as a friend to her old classmate, setting off hostilities.

● The Pavement Declarations: Risa and Ôtani become a couple!

● First Date: Risa tugs at Ôtani's heartstrings!!

A secret kiss behind everyone's backs! ♥

Second term

The Mimi Onslaught: A Beautiful Rival Attacks!

★ Ôtani's neighbor Mimi throws down the gauntlet!!

● Mimi declares love for Ôtani: Fiasco causes her to erupt at Risa.

● The Amusement Center Battle: Ôtani tries to give Mimi an answer.

● Mimi's Tantrum Attack → Risa retaliates with Meathead Punch → Mimi defeated.

Flanked by two tall beauties?

※3·4 Fireworks and Romance

Their second year, Risa tells Ôtani she loves him. Their third year, Ôtani kisses Risa. Do fireworks, with their beauty, noise and nighttime nature, abet romance?!

The Bambi Era

The "Learners Permit"

SECOND PERIOD BIOLOGY
See these once, they'll haunt your dreams...?
Illustrated diagram of Risa's many faces
Risa's expression is constantly changing to reflect how she feels. Here her various faces are analyzed in biological (?) terms!
• Animal 1 •
≪ Cat ≫
A mammal of the genus Felis. Size about 24 inches in length. The expression, "to pussyfoot around," means to move stealthily or to act cautiously. This, however, is something Risa cannot do.[1]
MEOWWW ♥
IS NOBU-CHAN A SEX KITTEN?!
Mammals
RISA KOIZUMI
EXPRES-SIVE GIRLS ARE SO VIVID AND LIVELY!
I THINK THEY'RE REALLY CHARM-ING.
In high spirits
I ♡ Mighty
WOW, SHE'S KINDA WOUND UP.
I CAN HARDLY BREATHE WHEN YOU LOOK AT ME LIKE THAT.
CAIN
WHO WOULD LOOK AT THIS AND EVER GUESS THAT THIS GIRL IS THE MAIN CHARACTER IN A SHOJO MANGA?
[1]information gathered from the Shueisha Dictionary

[2]information gathered from the Shueisha Dictionary

The drinks that make (some) people swoon with rapture!!

Tropical "Dancer" Recipes

Top-secret formulas leaked by disgruntled kitchen staff!

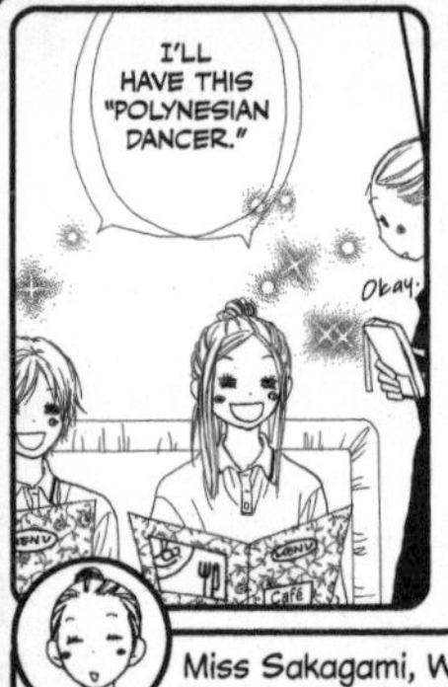

I'LL HAVE THIS "POLYNESIAN DANCER."
Okay.

What is a "Dancer"?

Background information

Tropical "Dancer" drinks are featured on the menu at Café Ikebe, the coffee shop where Risa and Ôtani always go. Their exotic names and interesting consistency have made them the talk of the town (?).

Miss Sakagami, Waitress

The "Dancer" series of drinks has been really popular ever since we introduced it. We come up with a new variation every season, so we hope you'll enjoy all of them!

LIGHT AND REFRESHING!

Let's make it!

Now it's your turn to try! Here's how you make the two tropical "Dancers" Risa and Ôtani had!!

One sip, and you're transported to the islands of King Kamehameha!

HAWAIIAN DANCER

DIFFICULTY ★

Ingredients (for one serving)

- 1/2 cup guava juice
- 1/2 cup lychee juice
- 1/2 cup lemon-lime soda
- 1 orange

Directions

1) Wash the orange thoroughly, then cut in half horizontally, make one slice to keep for decoration, and squeeze the rest.
2) Pour the fresh-squeezed orange juice into a shaker together with the guava and lychee juices, and shake well.
3) Pour the juice into a tall glass with lots of ice in it.
4) Top up with soda, and give a quick stir.
5) Decorate with the slice of orange.

A Little Tip!

To buy tropical juices, go to a liquor store!

Large discount liquor stores stock lots of imported fruit juices, also chocolates and other sweets!

IT'S FULL OF VITAMINS, AND IS REALLY GOOD FOR YOUR COMPLEXION.
IT IS? I NEVER NOTICED THAT ON YOU.

Directions

1) Peel the mango and remove the pulp from the seed with a knife. Or, don't peel it and slice along the seed, then use a spoon to scoop out the pulp.
2) Remove the nata de coco from its syrup and reserve the syrup.
3) Place the mango pulp, pineapple juice, coconut milk, milk and reserved syrup in a blender, and switch on!
4) When the ingredients have become smoothly blended, pour the mixture into a well-chilled glass.
5) Add the nata de coco and mix lightly.
6) Decorate with the pineapple slice, and serve!

Recipe 2

Close your eyes, and let the South Sea waves wash gently over you!

POLYNESIAN DANCER

DIFFICULTY ★★

A Little Tip!

It's also super-yum with banana!!

If you can't find ripe mangoes, try using a banana instead. It's really good, too. ☆ Since bananas turn brown quickly, sprinkle it with lemon juice as soon as you peel it, and then put it in the blender.

Ingredients
(for one serving)

- 1 mango
- 1/2 cup pineapple juice
- 1/2 cup coconut milk
- 1/2 cup milk
- 1/2 cup nata de coco (coconut jelly)
- 1 pineapple slice

In conjunction with Cafe Ikebe...

Have your recipe featured on the menu!

Wanted: Original "Dancer" Recipes!!

Café Ikebe is looking for exciting new drinks to feature on its menu as part of its "Dancer" series! Unique recipes that stimulate all five senses, baffling taste explosions, challenging new ideas—all are welcome! We look forward to receiving your recipes!

How to enter:
Write your 1) name 2) address 3) phone number 4) age 5) occupation and 6) original "Dancer" recipe (illustrations very welcome!) on a postcard, and send to the address below.
The recipe selected for the Grand Prix by the judging panel will be featured in the Café Ikebe menu.

Love Com "Dancer"
Recipe Contest
c/o Shojo Beat Magazine
295 Bay St
San Francisco,
CA 94133

We look forward to trying out your exciting ideas!

Café Ikebe
池辺 レストラン

Caution: Please forget all about this contest when you turn the Page!

LESSON2
Felt
Easy to make, and super-cute ♥
Usabarashi Coin Purse
Let's make the same coin purse that Risa lost and Umibôzu found in Hokkaido! Use the pattern at left, but first enlarge it by 130% on a copy machine.
Pattern included (enlarge by 130%)
What you'll need:
1 piece of red felt (8 inches square)
1 piece of white iron-on felt (7 inches square)
1 piece of yellow iron-on felt (7 inches square)
1 zipper (4 inches long)
1 skein each 6-strand embroidery thread* in red, yellow, and black
Embroidery needle
Pins
Sewing marker or chalk
*Divide each skein of 6-strand thread in half, and sew using 3 strands.
1 Cut out the pattern
Enlarge the patterns at left on a copy machine, to 130%.
Pin them onto the felt, and follow the lines to cut.
Iron the white and yellow pieces onto the red pieces.
<Patterns for iron-on felt>
Rabbits
(white, 1 set)
Stars
(yellow x 5)
Writing
(yellow, 10 letters)
USABARASHI
<Pattern for purse>
Cut two pieces like this out of the red felt.
(Diameter should be about 3.5 inches)
USE A SEWING MARKER OR CHALK TO DRAW A LINE AROUND 1/4 INCH INSIDE THE EDGE OF BOTH PIECES.

2 Embroider the design

Embroider the rabbits you ironed on in Step 1, following the instructions at left.

Use the backstitch to go all around the circle of red felt, along the line you drew in Step 1. Do this on both pieces of felt, using yellow thread.

<The rabbits' eyes>
Using black thread, bring the needle out from the backside of the felt to the front, tie a knot, and then bring the needle through to the backside again.

<Outlining the rabbits' mouths and teeth>
Use black thread to outline the mouths and teeth with the backstitch.

<Inside the mouths>
Use the red thread and the satin stitch for the inside of the rabbits' mouths.

<The right-hand rabbit's left arm>
Outline the left arm in black thread, using the backstitch.

Basic embroidery stitches

1) The Backstitch

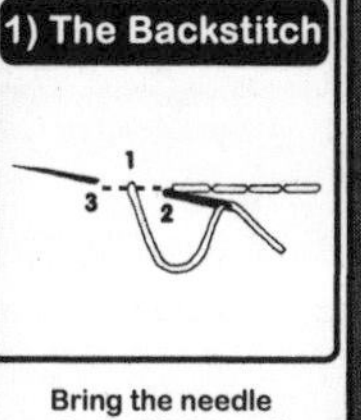

Bring the needle out a 2-stitch length from where it was inserted, go back 1 stitch, and repeat.

2) The Satin Stitch

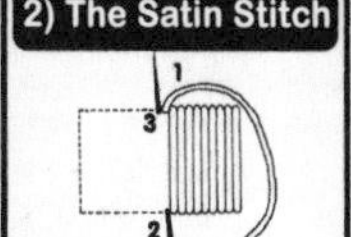

Place each stitch right next to the one before it to fill a space. Make sure you don't leave any spaces between stitches!

3) The Blanket Stitch

Place two pieces of fabric together. Bring the needle through from the front to the back, then pass it through the loop created and pull tight. Repeat.

3 Attach the zipper

Pin one half of the zipper onto the backside of the decorated piece of red felt, then sew it on with yellow thread, using the backstitch. Then pin the other half of the zipper onto the backside of the other piece of red felt and sew it on the same way. Make sure the zipper halves are facing the right way to zip up later!

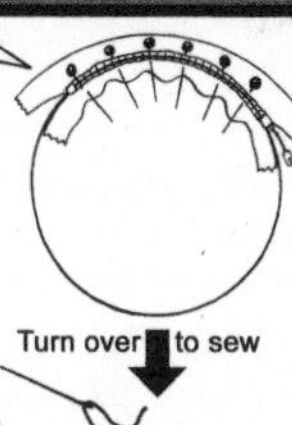

4 Sew the two sides together

Place the two pieces of red felt together and close the zipper. Then go all around the rest of the rim using the closing stitch.

FOR THE 1/2 INCH OR SO AT THE START AND GOAL SECTIONS, DOUBLE BACK ONCE AND THEN GO FORWARD AGAIN SO THE STITCHES ARE TRIPLE STRONG.
GOAL
START

How serious a fan are you? Find out with...

The Love★Com Details Test

Put away your Love Com graphic novels, and go!

Beginners' Level ★ Choose the correct answer. (1 point per question)

1 What is the current difference in Risa and Ôtani's heights?

1) 5 11/16 inches
2) 6 1/2 inches
3) 6 11/16 inches

2 What did Ôtani compare Risa to on the class trip to Hokkaido?

OKAY, SAY I TOLD YOU THAT, STARTING TODAY, YOU HAVE TO THINK OF THIS ? COULD YOU JUST GO, "OH, OKAY," AND THINK OF IT AS A CRAB?!
?
?

1) Pickled sour plum
2) Pickled radish
3) Pickled onion

3 Who was the black-suited assistant in the Basketball Team's skit?

1) Nakao
2) Giant Baba
3) Suzuki

4 What is Seiko's given name?

1) Seinosuke Kotobuki
2) Sei-ichirô Kotobuki
3) Seishirô Kotobuki

5 What did Risa give Ôtani for Christmas their second year of high school?

1) Gloves
2) Wristband
3) Ticket to Umibôzu show

6 Where did Risa and Ôtani go on their first date after becoming a couple?

THERE'S THIS PLACE I WANT TO CHECK OUT DOWNTOWN. MIND IF WE GO?
A PLACE YOU WANT TO CHECK OUT?

1) The beach
2) Karaoke
3) Game center

Intermediate Level

★ Fill in the blanks. (3 points per question)

1 Risa's birthday is on ______.

2 Risa's homeroom teacher is Mr. _____, more commonly known as _____. The subject he teaches is ______.

3 Mighty's real name is ______ ______. He is ___ years old.

4 The title of the dirty video Nakao had hidden in his room was _________.

5 _____ is the phrase Risa uses for shocks too big to say "Omigod."

6 Haruka is one-fourth ______.

7 Cain is a character in a game called ____________. His last name is ______.

8 Cain has _____ and café au lait for breakfast.

9 Hawaiian Dancer is on the menu of Café ______.

10 Their first year in school, Risa made Ôtani a Valentine's Day cake that said ________ on it.

11 At the School Festival their second year, Nakao dressed up as ______.

12 When Ôtani got sick with a fever, Risa brought him ______ when she went over to his house.

13 The color of the coin purse Risa dropped in Hokkaido was ______.

14 Ôtani is called ______ by his family.

15 For Ôtani's last basketball game, Risa made him lemons pickled in ______.

16 Risa called the dog pictured at right a _____ dog.

★ Choose the correct silhouette. (2 points)

17 Which of these is Umibôzu's signature hand signal?

THE
DVANCED
LEVEL'S
COMING
UP NEXT,
DUDES!

①

②

③

?

Advanced Level ★ Are the following statements true or false? Write T or F in the parentheses. (2 points)

1. Risa, Nobu and Chiharu all went to the same middle school.
2. Risa and Ôtani were in the same class for all three years of high school, and in Year 1 this was Class 2 and in Year 2 this was Class 4.
3. Both Nobu and Nakao have blood type B.
4. Haruka moved away in 4th grade.
5. According to the "Love Fortune" machine, Risa and Haruka are 38% compatible.
6. Mayu Kanzaki goes to Sakura Girls' School.
7. Ôtani was supplanted by Yamamoto as the basketball team's idol.
8. One of Umibôzu's CDs is called *Bozo.*

★ Choose the correct answer. (2 points per question)

9 What was the name of the beach Risa and the gang went to the summer of their second year?

THE BEACH!!
THE BEACH!!

1) Wakuwaku Beach
2) Tokimeki Beach
3) Tropical Beach

10 The show that was held at the beach that day was called "Rock the Boat and ???."

"ROCK THE BOAT
?
2002."
"UMIBÔZU AT TOKIMEKI BEACH."

1) Roll with the Punches
2) Make Some Waves
3) Fall Overboard

11 How many ear piercings does Haruka have?

Left ear
?
Right ear
?

1) One in his right ear, two in his left ear.
2) Two in his right ear, one in his left ear.
3) Two in each ear.

12 The wristband worn by Risa on the day before summer vacation her first year was which one below?

① ② ③

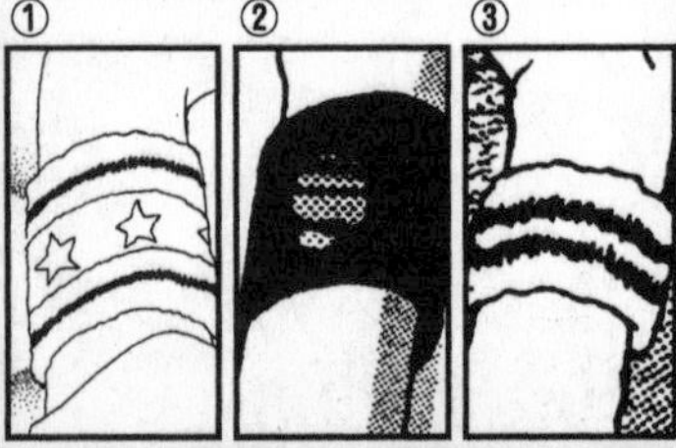

★Draw connecting lines between the two rows. (6 points)

13 Who went home with who at the end of that karaoke night?

A B C D E

F G H I J

★Find 7 differences between the two pictures at right. (2 points)

14

YOU'LL FIND ALL THE ANSWERS AT THE BACK!

UGH! WHAT THE HECK IS THIS?!

Welcome! We're the Mighty Girls

After-School Activities

MAITY♥

Main Activities

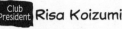

The Mighty Girls are here to cheer on our adored Mighty at all times, but in addition to that, we hold all kinds of special events! Teamwork is so important for cheering, and we practice really hard to make sure we're all together—because seeing Mighty smile when we're all in sync is sooo worth it! It's really easy to become a member: all you have to do is be crazy about Mighty!

I ♡ Mighty

Club President Risa Koizumi

Hi! We're a brand-new club so there's no hierarchy. We're all equals in our love for Mighty! So feel free to join us!

Meeting Places
Gymnasium (cheering)
Back courtyard (vocal exercises)
Audiovisual room (I-love-Mighty counseling)

Meeting Times
Mon-Fri after school at 3:30

Club Activities We start each session with vocal exercises!

Club Activities A Q&A session with the gorgeous man himself!

OKA IF YOU A QUES FOR MI RAISE HAN
ha ha ha
WOW, SO MANY PEOPLE HERE.
OVER HEEEERE

MAITY♥

OUR SHINING PRINCE ♥ MR. KUNIUMI MAITAKE

PROFILE

English teacher who is homeroom co-teacher for Risa's third-year class. Age 24. A Tokyoite who's new to Osaka. A real heartbreaker who made all the Mighty Girls cry—when they found out he has a fiancée! ♡

The Mighty Cheer

WITH THE MOVES!

JAPANESE SPELLING OF "MIGHTY"

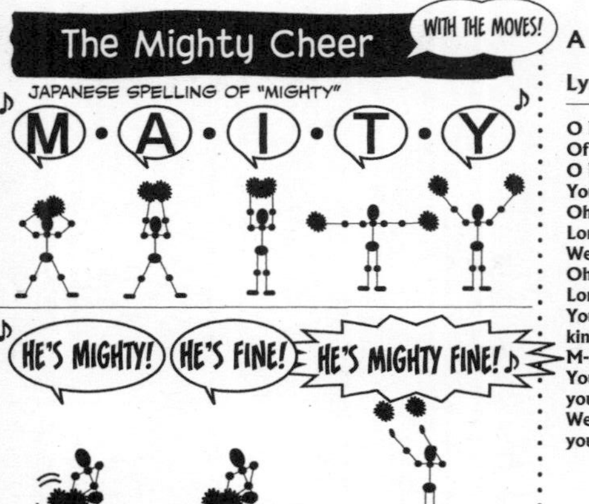

M · A · I · T · Y
HE'S MIGHTY!
HE'S FINE!
HE'S MIGHTY FINE!
Rotate arms → Bend knees → Jump up

SHOUT THIS CHEER OUT AT THE TOP OF YOUR LUNGS! IT'S SO ENERGIZING, YOU'LL FORGET ALL YOUR PROBLEMS!

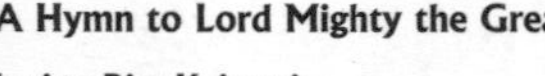

A Hymn to Lord Mighty the Great

Lyrics: Risa Koizumi

O Mighty your majesty
Of thee I sing
O Mighty, you rule
You are the king
Oh Mighty,
Lord Mighty
We're here to serve
Oh Mighty,
Lord Mighty
Your magical
kingdom of love
M-I-G-H-T-and-Y
You're Mighty,
you're fine
We love you cuz
you're divine!

SING THIS WHILE CLASPING YOUR HANDS TIGHTLY TOGETHER.

You too will fall for Mighty's many charms!!

↓You too will fall for Mighty's many charms!!

The Mighty Girls ♥

Paste photo here

NAME

BIRTH

BLOOD TYPE

As a Mighty Girl, I pledge to try and live an elegant life-style, and to love and adore Mighty forever and ever!

Since May 13, 2004

Membership #: mightygirl2004
Date joined:

All members get this special membership card!!

If you want to join, contact Risa Koizumi (3rd year)!!

Make these before you join!

POMPOMS

Wrap the pompom tape around the length of *Bessatsu Margaret* (or a phonebook, if *Bessatsu Margaret* is not available) about 100 times, then slip off and tie very tight around the middle. Cut the loops at both ends with scissors, then comb out to make them all fluffy! Repeat this process so you have two pompoms.

◇ What you'll need: 2 rolls Pompom tape 1 issue *Bessatsu Margaret* Scissors Wide-tooth comb

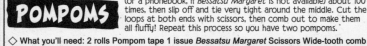

What did you think of the test? Was it a piece of cake? Super-hard? Now let's find out how you all did!!

<Beginners' Level> Q1: 3 Q2: 2 Q3: 1 Q4: 3 Q5: 1 Q6: 3

<Intermediate Level>

Q1: August 3rd
Q2: Nakano / Kong / Math
Q3: Kuniumi Maitake / 24
Q4: Titanic
Q5: Oh my gourd
Q6: English
Q7: Lovey-dovey Fantasia 2 / Osugi
Q8: Croissants
Q9: Ikebe
Q10: Just Friends
Q11: Rat Man
Q12: Tangerines
Q13: Red
Q14: Atchan
Q15: Cooking sherry
Q16: Yakuza
Q17: 3

<Advanced Level>

Q1: F (Risa and Chiharu did, but Risa only met Nobu on the first day of high school.)
Q2: F (They were in Class 3 their second year.)
Q3: T (Risa has O and Ôtani has A.)
Q4: F (He moved away in 5th grade.)
Q5: T (Chiharu and Suzuki's score was 18%.)
Q6: T (Sakura Girls' School students are supposed to be really smart.)
Q7: T (At first, Ôtani thought this was the guy Risa had a crush on.)
Q8: T (The others are Fish in Hell and Seasick.)
Q9: 2 Q10: 2 Q11: 1 Q12: 2
Q13: A-G, B-I, C-H, D-J, E-F
Q14: 1) Umibôzu 2) Crab 3) Nakao's wristband 4) The fish's mouth 5) Nobu's teeth 6) Suzuki's ribbon 7) Chiharu's swimsuit

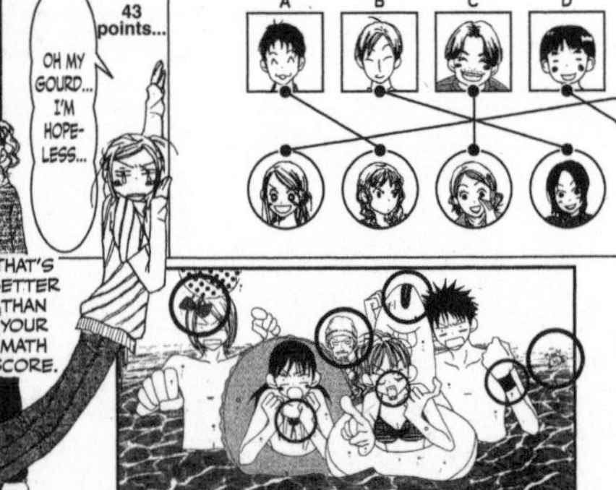

43 points...
OH MY GOURD... I'M HOPE-LESS...
THAT'S BETTER THAN YOUR MATH SCORE.

A B C D E

MIGHTY
Would you like to be charmed by me, my lady?

◀ Pinup of Mighty, Magician of Love. For luck in romance!

Illustrations: Aya Nakahara Planning: Caramel Mama Layout: Yasuhisa Kawatani

I Love You.

This happened right around the time Volume 7 [Japanese version] was released, so I couldn't tell you then, and now the timing's way off, but *Love★Com* has won a prestigious award called the Shogakukan Manga Award! This is all thanks to your warm support. Thank you all so much. I got really flustered and went to the ceremony flustered and came home flustered. I'll continue to work hard, flustered all the while, from now on.

Aya Nakahara won the 2003 Shogakukan manga award for her breakthrough hit *Love★Com,* which was made into a major motion picture and a PS2 game in 2006. She debuted with *Haru to Kuuki Nichiyou-bi* in 1995, and her other works include *HANADA* and *Himitsu Kichi.*

LOVE★COM VOL 8
The Shojo Beat Manga Edition

STORY AND ART BY
AYA NAKAHARA

Translation & English Adaptation/Pookie Rolf
Touch-up Art & Lettering/Gia Cam Luc
Design/Yuki Ameda
Editor/Pancha Diaz

Editor in Chief, Books/Alvin Lu
Editor in Chief, Magazines/Marc Weidenbaum
VP of Publishing Licensing/Rika Inouye
VP of Sales/Gonzalo Ferreyra
Sr. VP of Marketing/Liza Coppola
Publisher/Hyoe Narita

Printed in Canada

Published by VIZ Media, LLC
P.O. Box 77010
San Francisco, CA 94107

Shojo Beat Manga Edition
10 9 8 7 6 5 4 3 2 1
First printing, September 2008

Aishiteruze BABY™
By Yoko Maki
Kippei Katakura is a 17-year-old playboy, but when his 5-year-old cousin Yuzuyu comes to live with his family after her mother's sudden disappearance, Kippei is put in charge of taking care of her!
Shojo Beat Manga
Aishiteruze BABY
Aishiteruze Baby 1
Yoko Maki
Story & Art by
Yoko Maki
Only $8.99
Shojo Beat™

RATED
T+
FOR OLDER TEEN
ratings.viz.com